WHEN I WAS YOUR AGE

For my granddaughter Madison Crosse who inspired it and my daughter Lucy Crosse without whom it would never have been written

When I was your age

For my granddaughter in Australia
on her 18th birthday

Sheila Upjohn

The Larks Press

Published by the Larks Press
Ordnance Farmhouse
Guist Bottom
Dereham NR20 5PF

01328 829207

Larks.Press@btinternet.com

November 2010

Printed by Newprint and Design
Garrood Drive, Fakenham, Norfolk

British Library Cataloguing-in-Publication Data.
A catalogue record for this book is available
from the British Library.

ACKNOWLEDGEMENTS
The author wishes to thank Mr Jonathan Plunkett for permission to
reproduce the pictures on pp.98, 100, 109, 111, 114, & 118 which are taken
from George Plunkett's *Photographs of Old Norwich.*
The picture on p.56 is © TfL London Transport Museum collection.
The pictures on pages 116 &117 are reproduced by kind permission of the
Dean & Chapter of Norwich Cathedral. The pictures on pages 47 & 121 are
reproduced by kind permission of Letterbox Designs, Norwich.

ISBN 978 1 904006 55 8

CONTENTS

ILLUSTRATIONS

Dear Madison,

When I rang you in Sydney to ask what you'd
like for your eighteenth birthday, your reply astonished me:
'Please, Grandma, could you tell me what a day in your
life was like when you were a child growing up in
England? That's not easy. There are so many days to
choose from. How old was I? Was it winter or summer?
Was it school time or holidays? And is the day in the
first half or the second half of my childhood? That's
important because the first and second halves of my
childhood were very different from each other.

To give you a clue I'll tell you that I was born at the
end of 1930 so my first eighteen years ran through to
1949. I know you've studied the twentieth century as
history, but what I'm going to tell you about are the things
the history books don't think are important enough to
mention. And so instead of trying to choose a single day
I'll begin by telling you how every day began in the house
where I lived for the whole of my first eighteen years –
Dorset House, West Parade, Norwich, Norfolk, England.....

Dorset House

CHAPTER 1

The House where I was Born

As far back as I can remember, the first thing I'd hear in the morning is a knock at my parents' bedroom door and the chink of china. This means our maid Irene has left a tea-tray on the mat outside. *('What's this?' I hear you say. 'You had a servant!' Yes, we did. Nowadays I've heard people talk as though being a maid was a demeaning job, and that they were called 'skivvies', and badly treated. As I tell this story I hope you'll understand it wasn't like that, and how Irene became our lifelong friend and part of our family.)*

After my father has taken in the tea-tray he brings a cup to me and my two sisters, Thelma and Rosalind – who are eight and six years older than me. *(You'll remember when I stay with you in Sydney I still can't get up before I have a cup of tea in the morning.)* Then he goes to the bathroom to wash and shave. He shaves with a 'safety razor' and soap and water. Electric razors hadn't been invented. Then it is my mother's turn and finally the three of us pile in together.

We don't have to take turns in the shower as you do. We haven't got one. We just clean our teeth and wash our face and hands with Pears soap – which I still use today. There's a long story about our bathroom, but there's no time to tell you that now, because by eight o'clock we all have to be downstairs in the dining room for breakfast.

The table is laid with a starched white cloth and, if it is winter, a bright fire is burning. My mother rings the bell and Irene brings in a trolley with a silver teapot and hot water jug and bowls of porridge. You eat it with milk and can write your name on it with golden syrup. When we've finished, my mother rings the bell again and Irene takes the plates away and brings in toast and bacon and eggs. At half past eight my father drives off to work – he is wearing a tailor-made wool suit and a bowler hat. His office is fifteen minutes drive away. At twenty to nine my sisters walk down the road to school.

By the time I've waved them goodbye from the front gate my mother is in the kitchen talking to Irene, so it's a good time to show you round Dorset House. It's a tall grey-brick house that was built about 1820, and so it was over a hundred years old when we moved in 1930. *(I know that's very old in Australia, but it's not in England. In the*

Norfolk village where I live, some of the houses are two or three hundred years old.)

The front door is open – but first there are the front steps to negotiate. These are three wide stone steps, and Irene scrubs them every morning, and then rubs them over with a block of something called 'Hearthstone'. This looks very smart, as you can see, because it dries chalky white, but it also shows every footmark. I used to be very good at clearing the front steps at a bound, but I can't do that with my new hips, so you take a jump and I'll tiptoe and try not to leave a mark, so I don't 'get wrong' with Irene.

We find ourselves in a big square hall with a flight of stairs facing us, so we'll go up. There are fourteen steps, but the thirteenth creaks when you tread on it, so you have to step over it if you don't want anyone to hear you coming. We're on a landing with a corridor to the right leading to the bathroom and Irene's bedroom. The lavatory door is facing us, along to the left. So we turn left, and left again, and go up four more stairs. The third one creaks, so let's step over that one too.

Now we are outside the door to the bedroom I share with my sister Rosalind and next door to it is my parents' bedroom door, where Irene leaves the tea-tray in the morning. We turn left again, past my sister Thelma's bedroom door and facing us is the door to the guest bedroom, which is always called 'the big spare'. Opening off that is a small room we called 'the big spare bathroom cupboard'. I promised I'd tell you about bathrooms, and you'll be surprised to hear that when our house was built it didn't have a bathroom. And when my parents bought it in 1930 all it had was just this strange bathroom in a large cupboard. But at least it had water laid on, which was an improvement on the early days, when once a week the maids would carry hot water up from the kitchen and pour it into a hip bath (a sort of large enamel basin shaped like an armchair) in front of the bedroom fire. For their daily wash people would use the washstands in their bedrooms.

There's a washstand in 'the big spare' – I think it must have belonged to my grandmother. It is a kind of dressing table with a tiled top. A big china jug and basin stands there, plus a matching soap dish and mug. It is only used when my great aunt Julie (who is about a million years old and wears dangly earrings, weird long clothes and buttoned boots) comes to stay, and Irene has to take hot water up to her room.

In the cupboard below there's a matching china chamber pot – a big version of the plastic potties children use. It's a long time since you last used a potty, but in those days we all had enamel potties under our beds, including my parents. I suppose it was because both my parents had grown up in houses without an indoor lavatory and had never got out of the habit.

A lot of houses the same age as Dorset House still only had a lavatory in an outhouse. When I went to birthday parties at friends' houses we would often use the potty rather than go to the outside loo in our party shoes.

So before we moved in, my father had a proper bathroom installed, in what had been the second maid's bedroom – yes, when our house was built they thought it would need two maids to keep it clean. It is the room next to Irene's so we'll walk back and have a look.

The first thing you see is a large cast iron bath with a roll top and claw and ball feet. Over it is a gas geyser. It is called The Ewart and is a large copper cylinder with water pipes inside. There is a sign on the front in embossed copper letters: *GAS MUST BE TURNED OFF BEFORE ENTERING THE BATH.*

To get hot water, you turn on a stopcock, wait until the water comes through the system, light a pilot light with a match, and then turn it into the main cylinder. The gas then lights with a whoosh and soon afterwards the water coming through begins to get hot. If you don't have the water running fast enough it can turn to steam and the whole cylinder can explode.

Hot water was difficult to come by. The Ewart geyser was the latest thing, but it took ages to fill the bath and the Ideal boiler in the scullery, which heated the water in winter, sometimes went out and the water got cold. So, unlike you, who think nothing of showering two or three times a day, most people – including us – only had a bath once a week. And if you only have a proper wash once a week you want to make an occasion of it – not just pop in and out of it quickly.

Irene's parents, who lived in a little village called Rockland St Mary, certainly made an occasion of it. Irene told us that once a week she and her father, mother and two sisters would all have a bath in a big tin bath in front of the fire, with water heated up in a 'copper' in an outhouse and then scooped into the bath. The whole family would use the same water, one after the other – the youngest last. They didn't have mains water on tap, but had to draw it up in a bucket from a well in their garden. And of course they didn't have a flushing lavatory – just a seat with a hole in it in a shed in the garden and earth underneath.

9

This is just a quick look round Dorset House to let you get your bearings – and now it's time to go downstairs. Once upon a time we could have gone down the back staircase outside Irene's bedroom, which the maids used to get to and from the kitchen, but my father has had this taken out, so we'll go down the front one. I always used to slide down the banisters but it's probably safer if I walk this time.

Once we get into the hall and face the front door the drawing room is on our right. It's the 'best' room and we don't use it much except on Sunday afternoons and when people come to tea. It has a pink carpet with lilies on it, a lot of little occasional tables, two matching armchairs, and a sofa I'm not allowed to jump on. The piano is in there and both my sisters go in there to practise. It stands at an angle to the wall and I hide behind it when my mother is looking for me to give me a spoonful of Cod Liver Oil & Malt, or Milk of Magnesia, or – worse still – Slippery Elm Food.

Across the hall from the drawing room is the dining room where we have all our meals. I'll tell you about them later. It's got a dining table with six dining chairs, and an oak dresser with shelves full of blue and white china. Most of it is willow pattern – a Chinese scene with people crossing over a bridge. I used to wonder about the story behind it, and my father would recite:

If you take a willow pattern plate
and hold it in your hands
You'll see it's full from rim to rim
with scenes from foreign lands
You know it all means something,
and I'm going to relate
The sad and sorry story
of the willow pattern plate.

Unfortunately he didn't know any more – and I thought I'd never find out who the people were, why they were crossing the bridge and where they were going.

(Madi! I've just googled it and now I know the whole sad story, and even the rest of my father's forgotten poem – after waiting more than 70 years. Isn't the internet wonderful!)

There are a couple of armchairs beside the fire, a bureau with a shelf of books below it and a gramophone cabinet with a silver biscuit barrel and fruit bowl on top. A gramophone cabinet is a piece of furniture with a lift-up lid and a turntable inside that plays those big old black records. There's a handle coming out of the side to wind it up. If you don't wind it up in time, the record goes slower and slower and the tone of the music gets deeper and deeper – a bit different from your iPod. We could leave the dining room by a door beside the fireplace, which my father has just knocked through the wall, and go into the kitchen. But instead we'll go back into the hall, turn right and walk along the hall until we come to the nursery.

This is where I spend most of my time. There's a fireguard with a brass top rail in front of the fire, which is sometimes used for airing clothes. There's a sideboard where we keep our toys and a big dining room table, which you can make even bigger by slotting in leaves. I think they both must have belonged to my grandmother. We turn the table upside down to make a ship, and drape table cloths over to make a den. Right side up, we hang curtains from the picture rails and use it as a stage. We play table tennis and tap dance on it. We make slides from the extra leaves and build more dens with them.

Years later a friend showed me what she said was a William IV dining table which she had bought in an antique shop at enormous expense. I'm pretty sure it was our old nursery table – but I didn't tell her. When we go out of the nursery, the back door of the house, where the tradesmen call, is on our left and the cellar door is opposite. We'll leave the cellar till later, and turn right and then left into the kitchen.

Once there had been an iron kitchen range in the kitchen, a big black cooking stove with an enclosed fire – the sort of stove my grandmother used to cook on – but my father has had it replaced by a modern version called a Triplex with an open fire burning brightly. The base of an old dresser stands against one wall and on it there's a big copper kettle on a stand with a spirit lamp under it – something else of my grandmother's.

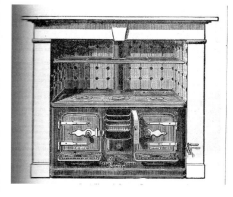

Above the kitchen door is a bell board with numbered labels that move to show which bell has been rung in which room. Every room, upstairs and down, has a bell-push beside the fireplace. I've told you how my mother rings the bell in the dining room when she wants Irene to come and clear the plates and bring the next course. We also ring for her when the fire needs making up. We ring for her again when the big brass coal scuttle is empty, and she goes down to the cellar and fills it up. It sounds dreadfully lazy to me now, but this is the way things were done.

The bell board is also connected to the bells at the front and the back doors. In those days people did not answer the front door themselves. When you rang the front door bell a maid would open it, and you then had to ask: 'Is your mistress in?' This was quite handy, because if you did not want to see someone you could tell the maid to say you were 'not at home'. You don't even have a bell on your front door. People just give a shout and walk in.

Opening off the kitchen is a larder where we keep our food and a big china pantry. The china pantry is a small room with lots of shelves where we keep the china and glass. There's a big stone jar of ginger beer in there as well. It now has shelves on one side, instead of three, because it is directly behind the dining room and my father has had a door put through. This means Irene doesn't have to go all the way round by the hall to get to the dining room, as the maids have been doing for the last hundred years.

The kitchen is a cosy place. My sisters and I spend a lot of evenings sitting round the kitchen fire with Irene. We take our books and our knitting. Irene is good at picking up dropped stitches. We sometimes listen to the wireless – a radio serial called The Count of Monte Cristo and the Ovalteenies, a programme sponsored by Ovaltine, which must have been on the only commercial channel, Radio Luxemburg.

The scullery leads off the kitchen and is where most of the work is done. It has a brick floor covered by coconut matting. This is made of some kind of coarse rope-like stuff – perhaps it really is made from coconut fibre. There's a deep china sink with a wooden draining board. It's called a 'Belfast sink' – they're back in fashion now. In one corner there's a grey enamel 'Ideal' boiler, which heats the water. It burns coke (which is hard dry fuel left over from the coal that's been used to make gas) not coal like the ordinary fires. Before natural gas was discovered in the North Sea there was a big gasworks just across the road from Norwich cathedral. It used to belch out clouds of sulphur-smelling smoke – which can't have been very good for the cathedral's stonework.

There's a large black gas cooker which has four gas jets and a grill on top, all of them emerging from black pipes. These get covered in grease and are terribly difficult to clean. Every so often they have to be disconnected and the whole lot soaked in some very strong stuff called caustic soda. *(Now I cook on a sheet of solid glass that just has to be wiped over.)* The oven does not have any way of regulating the heat. You just have to keep an eye on what is happening and turn the gas up or down if you think it needs it. It's a bit different from your new oven, which has eight different functions and tells you what the temperature is inside the joint of meat while it is cooking – and even cleans itself.

The back door of the scullery opens into the kitchen yard, so we'll walk across and open the doors of the outhouse on the other side. In the first one there's the mangle which we use mainly on Monday – washing day – next there's the outside lavatory – it has a stone floor and is rather damp, with lots of woodlice and spiders (at least they're not funnel-webs) and a bit scary – and then there's the big brick cupboard where the dustbin lives.

Being a dustman was a pretty smelly job in those days. We didn't have plastic bins and put them on the road, like you do in Australia, and we didn't recycle anything. All the waste – potato peelings, tea leaves, food scraps, empty tins, bottles and paper – was just thrown into a galvanised bin. A few bottles got re-used, and you got a penny back if you returned them. And plastic bags weren't a problem because we didn't have any. Plastic hadn't been invented.

The dustmen walked round the house with big metal bins on their shoulders and emptied our dustbin into their containers. Then they chucked the contents into the dustcart, jumped onto a ledge at the back and were driven away, hanging on to a rail, with all the smelly stuff reeking in front of them. But they seem very cheerful and are always whistling.

One day, when they were emptying our bin, Irene was cooking a joint of pork in the Triplex oven. When the fire was alight in winter we often used the Triplex instead of the gas oven. She opened the door to see how it was getting on and a sheet of flame shot up to the ceiling. She screamed – she would have said 'shruck out' – slammed the door, and held it shut with a broom. One of the dustmen saw what was happening. He jumped through the window, seized a fire extinguisher, flung open the oven door and squirted the stuff all over the inside. It put the fire out, and we had bread and cheese for dinner.

CHAPTER 2

Semolina & Suet

Bread and cheese for dinner meant that something had gone wrong because, like most people in those days, we ate our main meal at home

together in the middle of the day. Schools did not supply food and nobody took sandwiches. There were hardly any restaurants or cafés. The big shops in Norwich – Jarrolds, Curls and Buntings – each had a restaurant on the top floor where my mother and her friends would go for morning coffee. Then there were 'tea rooms' – often run by unmarried ladies – but all of these served 'light meals' not substantial dinners.

Hotels like the Maid's Head (pictured) would serve a midday meal – something like Brown Windsor Soup, followed by Roast Beef with two vegetables and Apple Pie and Custard – but no one would have dreamed of going there for their everyday meal.

When I stay with you in Sydney I am amazed by the number of different sorts of restaurants we can choose from. There's Indian, Chinese, Vietnamese, Thai, Lebanese, Mexican, French, German, Greek, Italian, Japanese, Mongolian – and I've probably missed a few. It's because Australia is made up of so many nationalities and they all bring their cooking skills with them. In Norwich in my childhood there were very few people who had not been born and bred there. Anyone from outside Norfolk was thought of as a 'foreigner' and even the fact that my parents came from London made me feel a bit of an outsider.

The only real foreigners who had become established in Norwich were some Italians who had settled there about the beginning of the century. They had names like Peruzzi, Valori and Carrara and they mostly lived in Ber Street. We used to hear there were fights up there on a Saturday night, but I don't know if it's true. A lot of them sold ice cream or owned fish and chip shops. We sometimes had fish and chips, but we nearly always had home-cooked English food. *(If my mother had given my father sushi and told him he was expected to eat rice and raw fish wrapped in seaweed he would have thought she had taken leave of her senses.)*

Thelma and Rosalind would get back from school about quarter to one and my father got home at one o'clock. Even when my sisters had left school and started work, they would still cycle back home for a midday meal. So at one o'clock everything for a proper meal had to be ready to put on the table.

Meals really were 'proper' then. They began with grace ('For what we are about to receive may the Lord make us truly thankful') and there was something called 'table manners'. We had to sit up straight and not put our elbows on the table. We weren't allowed to talk with our mouths full. We had to put our knife and fork down on our plate when we weren't using them, and when we had finished we had to put them side by side and ask 'Please may I get down?'

On Monday we had a 'makeshift' meal, which was cold meat left over from the Sunday joint, because it was washing day. On the other days we had things like stew, fish, sausages, chops, shepherds pie, liver (horrible!), steak and kidney pudding (which is made with suet pastry and boiled in a pudding basin) – all ordinary English food. On Sundays we had a roast – beef or pork or lamb. But the real treat was chicken. Chicken were not intensively reared like the ones you eat today. They were expensive and bigger and had much more flavour – absolutely delicious.

(I loved getting the 'wish-bone', a V-shaped piece of bone which you have to crook your finger through and pull with someone else until it breaks. If you get the bigger piece, you make a wish. Although I always buy free-range, chicken are eaten when they're so young they scarcely seem to have bones – more like gristle these days.)

We never had spaghetti (though there was macaroni cheese which I loathed), or curry, or nachos or pizza or any other of the food you take for granted. It was not possible to buy garlic peppers, sweet corn, yams, aubergines and lots of other food – and of course you can't grow these in England. For pudding we would have stewed fruit, or apple pie, or rice pudding or bread and butter pudding. *(You make this by putting slices of stale bread and butter into a dish, sprinkling them with currants and then pouring milk and beaten egg over it before baking it in the oven.)*

We sometime had salad, which meant lettuce, cucumber and tomatoes. There was also beetroot, soaked in vinegar, and radishes. There was only one sort of lettuce which had floppy leaves, and had to be washed very carefully to get rid of the earth and insects. (Nothing was grown by hydroponics then.) We had never heard of iceberg or cos lettuce, let alone radicchio – and we would never have thought of using spinach or beetroot leaves or rocket. We had to make the salads ourselves – you could not buy bags of mixed salad as you can today. The only salad dressing we had was Heinz Salad Cream. You couldn't buy ready-made mayonnaise. No one had heard of oil and vinegar dressing. The only vinegar we had was brown malt vinegar – there was no wine vinegar, cider vinegar, balsamic vinegar or any of the others people take for granted now.

Nowadays, like you, I buy olive oil in three-litre cans. We did have olive oil in our larder. It was a little bottle that held about a cupful. I only remember it being used once, when I had earache, and they put a tiny spoonful of warmed olive oil into my ear. *I don't think it did any good.* We never used oil for cooking. Our cooking was done in lard – which is animal fat – or in dripping from the meat. I think the bought fish and chips were cooked in lard, not oil, too. They came in a small greaseproof bag, wrapped in newspaper.

It seems very ungrateful of me, but what I remember most is the food I disliked – mainly the puddings. There was something ghastly called semolina, a sort of white mush with a gritty texture. Then there was tapioca, a sticky white glue – absolutely revolting. And rice pudding – a little better but not much. Rice was only ever used for puddings, never instead of potatoes or in risotto or salad. Custard could be pretty grim too, because it developed a yucky skin. Worst of all were 'swimmers'. These were dumplings made from flour and suet, with a few currants added. *(Suet is hard white fat that surrounds ox kidney. You can't even get it in supermarkets in Australia now.)*

'Swimmers' were boiled in water and had a glutinous slimy skin. You were supposed to eat these with golden syrup. I say 'supposed to eat them' because I wouldn't. I have a lot of early memories of sitting in my high chair for ages at the dining table with a plate of one or other of these revolting dishes in front of me. I was meant to sit there until I ate it – but I never did.

My mother seemed to spend her life trying to make me eat things I didn't like. The trouble was that it was fashionable in those days to have children with round rosy cheeks and dimples, like Shirley Temple. My sisters and I were naturally skinny and my mother kept trying to fatten us up. (*No one talked about obesity in those days. During the depression of the nineteen thirties a lot of people were thin because they didn't have enough to eat.*) My mother's oldest sister Auntie Grace had a daughter called Norma who was 'nice and plump' (I thought she was fat) and my mother was upset because her own daughters looked under-fed. She finally gave up when an osteopath – bless him – said: 'Have you ever tried to fatten a greyhound? These children are racehorse breed' and after that things got better.

If I were to ask you to put a proper meal on the table at midday you could do it without too much trouble. You could heat up a ready-meal in the microwave, or you could simply get something from a takeaway. There weren't any microwaves and there weren't any takeaways – apart from fish and chips – in Norwich in my childhood. And there were no frozen foods of any kind – no ready meals, no prepared chips, no frozen vegetables. Everything had to be prepared from scratch. Peas came in pods and had to be shelled – I used to sit on the scullery doorstep with a big bowl of peas and shell them into a colander – and potatoes had to be peeled. I don't think we ever had a meal that did not include potatoes.

There was no frozen pastry to make the apple pies and there were no food processors. Making pastry took quite a long time, as you had to rub the butter and lard into the flour with your hands until it looked like breadcrumbs, then add water and roll it out. It was also messy and got flour all over the floor and the kitchen table.

Usually when we came home from school we would have tea round the dining room table. As well as bread and butter, cakes and biscuits, we would have something like beans on toast or sardines on toast. Sometimes we would make toast on the fire by holding a piece of bread on a toasting fork near the glowing coals. (There weren't any pop-up toasters.) My parents would have a meal later on.

17

I don't think that people in Sydney have afternoon tea any longer – though I've had wonderful cake and sandwiches for 'morning tea' – and I don't know many people in England who do either, but when I was a child it seemed to be the time to entertain. When friends were invited we would have afternoon tea in the drawing room. This took a lot of preparation. There were plates of bread and butter – brown and white. Sliced bread had not been invented, and in any case the bread had to be cut very thinly. *(My mother would have called slices the thickness of today's sliced bread 'doorsteps'.)* To get really thin slices you have to have the butter the right temperature and use a very sharp knife which you put in a jug of very hot water after cutting each slice. Some were made into sandwiches, with the crusts cut off and two or three different sorts of filling – salmon and shrimp paste or sardines or grated cheese or Marmite. Other slices were left plain for jam.

There would be three or four different sorts of homemade jam in little glass dishes, biscuits and several sorts of cakes. These were all homemade. We had a piece of furniture called a cake stand that held three plates of cakes, one above the other. The cake plates were covered by linen doilies – a piece of cloth with handmade lace or crochet round the edges. We used thin embroidered table napkins – not the big white ones we used in the dining room. All these had to be washed by hand, starched and ironed afterwards. We used a special tea set with thin china cups and saucers.

Some of the people who came to tea were our neighbours in West Parade and it's time to go out and meet them.

CHAPTER 3

Friends & Neighbours

There were thirty houses in West Parade, and we knew all our neighbours. We could keep an eye on their comings and goings too, because West Parade is a cul-de-sac and Dorset House is at the top, so our dining room window was a wonderful vantage point.

Our next door neighbours were Dr Muriel and his sister Miss Muriel. Dr Muriel, a retired consultant from the Norfolk and Norwich Hospital, was a widower, and his sister kept house for him. He was a stout man with gold-rimmed glasses. Miss Muriel was thin and very upright and wore a lot of lace and gold chains. Their house smelt of furniture polish and lavender. Hanging from the banisters was a set of cow bells, which they had brought back from Switzerland, *(not many people had been to Switzerland in those days)* which tinkled when you walked past.

The Muriels had two maids – a cook and a housemaid. Miss Muriel's job of 'keeping house' meant that she would decide the menus for the day with the cook each morning and tell her what to order. She would keep the household accounts and pay the bills (with Dr Muriel's money). She would supervise the maids, to see the work was done properly, and she would act as hostess when they entertained.

(That phrase 'supervise the maids' reminds me of hearing two grown-ups during the war who were discussing how they would manage afterwards, when there would be no maids to cook for them. 'I shall be perfectly all right,' said one. 'I can boil an egg, and I can superintend the cooking of a chop.' I imagine that superintending the cooking of a chop would have been the limit of Miss Muriel's culinary accomplishments.)

As well as the maids, the Muriels had a gardener/chauffeur whose name was Buck – a big man with strong hands and a kind smile. He spoke with a Norfolk accent, like Irene. The Muriels needed a chauffeur because although they had a car – an Armstrong Siddley with a silver sphinx on the bonnet – neither of them knew how to drive.

The car had brown leather seats and there was a glass screen between the front and back seats. Buck wore a chauffeur's uniform with a peaked cap when he drove them, and Miss Muriel spoke to him through a speaking tube to tell him where they wanted to go.

Buck kept the garden immaculate. There were no weeds in the flower beds and the lawn was so smooth that they used it as a bowling green. Their friends used to come once a month to play bowls – but they didn't dress up in white, as people do in Australia. You might find it unusual for a brother and sister to keep house together, but one of the things you'll notice about those days is that, if children did not marry, they stayed together as a family when they were grown up.

None of the children in the Osborne family, who lived on the other side of us, had got married.

The household consisted of old Mrs Osborne and two daughters called Daisy and Mabel. Another daughter was a nun and appeared from time to time dressed all in black with a complicated lace frill round her face. There was also a rather mysterious son. He never used the front door in West Parade, but used to go out by the back gate which led into Mill Hill Road. He wore a brown felt hat and always walked fast with his head bent so you could not see his face, and if you met him in the street he never spoke or looked at you.

I think the Osbornes had once been well off, but now seemed to have very little money and wore strange old-fashioned clothes, some of which they seemed to have made themselves, rather inexpertly. They used to 'keep themselves to themselves' and we never thought we would get to know them.

But we did, very well, a few years later.

Next door to them lived another family that had stayed together – old Mrs Rivett and her daughter Miss Rivett. And in the next house lived another brother and sister – Mr Bryant and his sister Miss Bryant. They ran a business selling ladies' clothes and their front room was fitted with built-in wardrobes with mirror fronts. His name was Frank and he called the business by the French version of his name – Francois. But most Norfolk people could not pronounce it and I kept meeting people walking up and down West Parade asking which house was Frankoys. *(I thought it would have been sensible if he'd called himself Pierre, even if his name wasn't Peter.)*

There were only three other families with children in West Parade. Their surnames all begin with B – Boswell, Barker and Boston. The Boswells lived near the bottom of West Parade and had two boys Graham and Barry. Mrs Boswell was very elegant. She was always beautifully dressed and her make-up was perfect.

The older boy, Graham, was almost grown up, but Barry used to come and play with us. He was a sturdy boy with thick dark hair who wore grey flannel shorts, kept up with a belt with a snake on it, and a white open-necked shirt. The highlight of my three-year old life was the afternoon I was married to Barry, dressed in an old lace curtain from the airing cupboard, with a big brass curtain ring for a wedding ring.

Sometimes a man pushing a barrel organ – which played a tune when he turned the handle – would come up West Parade and we would get off our bikes and run inside to get some money to give him.

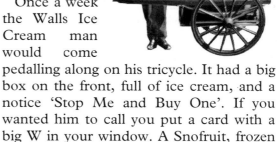

Once a week the Walls Ice Cream man would come

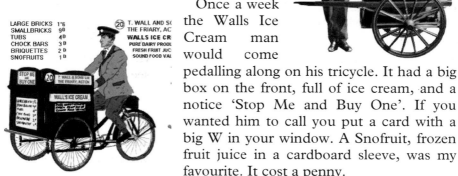

pedalling along on his tricycle. It had a big box on the front, full of ice cream, and a notice 'Stop Me and Buy One'. If you wanted him to call you put a card with a big W in your window. A Snofruit, frozen fruit juice in a cardboard sleeve, was my favourite. It cost a penny.

The Barkers' house still had a back staircase, meant for the maids to use. It was great fun rushing up one staircase and down the other – and very useful for hiding when you were playing Hide and Seek, or Murder, or Squashed Sardines. *(Squashed Sardines is like Hide and Seek, except, when you find the person, you join them in the hiding place. And in Murder the 'murderer' pinches someone in the dark and the 'detective' has to question everyone to find out who did it. The only person allowed to tell a lie is the 'murderer'.)*

The other games we played were charades – where you act out the syllables of a word which the others have to guess – and the drawing game Pictionary. We played chess, and draughts, and Halma, and Monopoly (which had just been invented). We also played Kim's Game where you put a lot of things on a tray and have to memorise them so that, later, you know what has been taken off. We didn't have computer games, and if you played Solitaire or any other sort of Patience you had to do it with real cards.

Our outdoor games were deck tennis, badminton, croquet, leapfrog, hopscotch and some complicated skipping games. We also had a swing and a seesaw that my father had made, and we played tennis on courts at a nearby park. We only swam when we went to the sea 20 miles (32km) away, because we didn't have a pool. Hardly anybody in England did then – and not many do now. It's too cold.

In the autumn we didn't celebrate Halloween and go round door to door getting sweets, as you did when you were younger. We had Guy Fawkes night on 5th November instead. *(You probably haven't heard of Guy Fawkes so I'll have to explain that he tried to blow up the Houses of Parliament in 1605 but was caught just in the nick of time. From that day on everyone in England has a bonfire on 5th November and burns a 'guy' on top of it.)*

As Guy Fawkes night drew near we used to stuff an old pair of pyjamas with straw to make a 'guy', put a hat on him and then push him up and down West Parade in my old pushchair shouting 'Penny for the Guy' and chanting:

Please to remember
The fifth of November
Gunpowder, treason and plot,
For I see no reason
Why gunpowder treason
Should ever be forgot.

I don't remember getting any pennies, but it was fun. Then on 5th November we'd invite our friends and light a bonfire in our garden and put the guy on top of it and watch him burn. Then we'd let off lots and lots of fireworks. They were nothing like the amazing firework displays I've watched with you on Sydney Harbour on New Year's Eve, but it was exciting letting off Roman Candles and Rockets and Catherine Wheels and Silver Rain and Jumping Jacks in the garden on a frosty November night. Then we'd all go inside and light sparklers and have hot soup and sausages.

You have to go to the Blue Mountains or the Snowy Mountains if you want to see snow, but in winter we often had deep snow in our garden – sometimes for weeks at a time. We used to build snowmen, have snowball fights and go tobogganing. And there was so little traffic in those days it was quite safe to take our toboggan out onto the roads and slide down hills there.

Our friend Fay Boston lived near the bottom of West Parade, almost opposite the Boswells. The Boston's house was full of dark furniture and they had two grandfather clocks. One had orbs showing the phases of the sun and the moon. The other had a dark oak case with these words carved on it:

I serve thee with all my might
And tell the hours both day and night
Therefore example take by me
And serve thy God as I serve thee

The Bostons had a golden cocker spaniel called Major, who I think was a bit of a disappointment to Fay's mother, who had bought him as a pet for Fay. Cocker spaniels are one-man dogs, and Major adored Mr Boston and hardly looked at the rest of the family.

Most of the fathers in West Parade were remote people who just went off to 'business' in the mornings, but Mr Boston's job was much more interesting because he was a jeweller and pawnbroker. You probably don't know what a pawnbroker is, because nowadays if people want a loan they go to a bank, but in those days a lot of people did not have a bank account, and if you wanted a loan you got money from a pawnbroker. The system is this: you take something of value – say a watch, or a piece of silver, or a fur coat – to the pawnbroker. He keeps it, and gives you a loan representing a percentage of the value, plus a pawn ticket which you hand over when you repay the money. If you can't raise the money to repay the loan he keeps the goods. Mr Boston's shop was right by the Cattle Market in Norwich where, every Saturday, farmers from all over Norfolk would come into Norwich to buy and sell, and I expect quite a few of them got into one of the many public houses all round the market and afterwards found themselves a bit short of ready cash – so his shop was very well placed.

A pawnbroker's shop has three brass balls outside and is sometimes called the 'pop shop' because when you pawn something you 'pop' it. One of the songs we used to sing was

Half a pound of tuppenny rice
Half a pound of treacle
That's the way the money goes
Pop goes the weasel!

Up and down the City Road
In and out the Eagle
That's the way the money goes
Pop goes the weasel!

We didn't realise at the time that the Eagle is a pub in the City Road in London and the weasel is a fur coat. So 'Pop goes the weasel' means they've had to pawn the wife's fur coat – yet again.

CHAPTER 4

Life without Jeans

My mother didn't have a fur coat but she did have a fox fur stole. This is something very grisly indeed – a dead fox which you drape round your shoulders. The body has been opened out and lined with satin and the fox's face has glass eyes put into it. A spring has been fixed in its jaw to make it open and shut, so it can snap onto another part of its body. My mother used to wear this sometimes when she went out to coffee with her friends. I thought it was wonderful and used to dress up in it, and put on one of her hats, and clonk about in her high-heeled shoes.

It seems unbelievable these days that anyone would wear such a gruesome garment, but in those days wearing fur was thought very fashionable. Some coats were made from silver fox, which were kept in cages. There was a silver fox farm at Taverham just outside Norwich and I once was taken to see them. *(They were pacing up and down in their cages, and they were smelly.)* People also wore coats and collars made of ocelot and leopard skin and sealskin – all of which had been hunted and shot. I'm glad nobody wears fur nowadays. In any case it's too hot in Australia – though you do wear sheepskin Ugg Boots. But those skins come from sheep that would have ended up as roast lamb in any case – and not from animals that were hunted and shot, or shut up in cages all their lives.

The fur fox stole was kept in the wardrobe in my parents' bedroom. This was not built-in but was a separate piece of furniture – a cupboard with a mirrored door, with a rail about two feet long running from front to back at each side of it. Remembering it makes me realise how few clothes we had then, compared with today. My parents shared a wardrobe, and this was all the hanging space they had. My sister Rosalind and I also shared a wardrobe, and we had about the same amount of space. I should think the hanging space in your bedroom is about four times that amount, just for one person, and I now have a walk-in wardrobe that's enormous.

Our shoes were all kept in a deep drawer underneath. Nobody had many pairs of shoes in those days. You know I'm mad on detective stories and I've just been reading one of the Maigret books written in the 1970s where the detective, after searching a suspect's flat, says:

'She must have a thing about shoes, because we found no less than eight pairs.'

We had outdoor shoes, and a pair of indoor shoes that were kept at school. You don't need these in Australia, but England is often so wet that wearing outdoor shoes would tramp mud all over the school. We had wellington boots for wet weather, sandals for summer and a pair of party shoes. For gym and tennis we wore 'plimsolls' with rubber soles and canvas tops – and that was all. Trainers and thongs had not been invented. Like the rest of our clothes, our shoes were made of natural materials – leather uppers with either leather or rubber soles. Leather soles wear out and have to be repaired. There was a cobbler in Earlham Road, near the bottom of West Parade. He was a small wrinkly man with gold-rimmed glasses and wore a brown cotton overall. As you stepped down the steep steps into his little shop, a lovely tinkly bell on a spring told him you were there.

My mother and her friends wore silk stockings. These are very delicate and ladder easily. I imagine they must have been very expensive because my father would buy her a dozen pairs of silk stockings for her birthday every year. (I don't think he ever went into the shop himself. He used to ask Thelma to buy them when she was old enough and before that I imagine he must have sent his secretary.) Because silk stockings laddered so easily you had to put them on very carefully, rolling them up as you went, not just pull them on, like nylons. Most people wore artificial silk or lisle (a kind of thin wool) for every day.

Stockings were made flat and then sewn together, not knitted as a tube as they are now, and they had a seam at the back. It was very important to have the seams running straight up the back of your legs and, before she went out, my mother – and my sisters when they were older – would often ask 'Are my seams straight?'

The older girls at my first school used to wear black woollen stockings in winter and fawn lisle stockings in summer. They were thick and went wrinkly at the ankle. Younger children wore white cotton ankle socks in summer and fawn woollen knee socks (kept up with elastic garters) in winter. Mixing synthetics with a fabric makes it more durable, but our pure wool and cotton stockings and socks used to wear out at the toes and heels and my mother used to stretch the sock over a mushroom-shaped piece of wood and darn them as she sat by the fire in the evenings. *(I don't suppose you know what darning is, Madison. You thread a long darning needle with wool to match the sock and sew strands of wool across the hole. Then you turn the sock round and sew more strands across at right-angles, weaving them in and out of the first lot. If you're good at it, you make a neat patch. Once when I tried to darn a sock for him, my father said it looked more like camouflage netting.)* Because tights had not been invented, keeping stockings up was a problem.

My mother used to wear corsets. These were not the sort her own mother used to wear – she told me her mother would hang on to the bedpost while my grandfather tugged to lace her into it – *just see how small her waist is in the photograph in chapter 11.* My mother's corsets were a sort of body belt with suspenders attached. They were made of thick pink cotton that did up with laces and with hooks and eyes, and she had to struggle

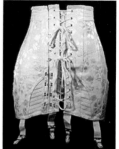

into them. In winter she wore a thin woollen vest and a silk petticoat over that. She never wore a bra. I think these came in sometime during the 1930s.

My sisters used to wear elastic 'roll-ons', and when I was about twelve I had a suspender belt to keep my stockings up. Before that I, and the rest of my friends, wore a strange garment called a 'liberty bodice'. This was a sort of thick cotton vest which had rubber buttons at the bottom. Suspenders buttoned on to these and stockings on to the suspenders. If you wanted to pull your stockings up, you simply shrugged your shoulders.

You may find this hard to believe, but my father wore suspenders, too. Socks in those days were made of pure wool and sagged round your ankles. So my father used to wear garters with suspenders attached to keep them up. And he wore elastic braces to keep his trousers up, too.

A lot of our summer clothes didn't look much different from today (some of the school uniforms I see in Sydney look as if they've stepped straight out of the 1930s). We had cotton dresses, and shirts and shorts. But they did up with buttons, press studs, or hooks and eyes, not zip fasteners. Velcro had not been invented.

Winters are much colder in England and we used to get very cold, too. There were no fleece-lined windcheaters or anoraks. I used to wear a tweed overcoat or my gabardine school mackintosh in the snow, with lots of woollen jumpers underneath. Girls did not wear trousers and there were no thick tights to keep you warm. I wore a skirt and knee socks, and still remember the feeling of snow seeping over the tops of my wellington boots and freezing my bare knees. Boys did not wear long trousers until they were about 12, and until then they wore shorts all winter.

Can you imagine your life without jeans? Nobody wore them then. Perhaps a few cowboys wore them in the Wild West – like the ones in the picture on the Levi Strauss label where they've hitched a pair of jeans between two horses and are trying to pull them apart – but they certainly weren't a fashion item. In fact very few women wore trousers, and my mother never owned a pair in her whole life.

My mother used to make quite a lot of our clothes, and our costumes for dressing up. Her sewing machine, which they'd bought second-hand when they got married in 1917, folded down into a cabinet and was worked by a treadle – an iron platform which you rock to and fro with your feet. The machine only went forwards and did straight stitch, but you could alter the length of the stitches. It's a far cry from your computerised sewing machine that can do an amazing variety of stitches, but it was very serviceable and satisfactory. *(If you own one in a third world country you can still make a living with it.)*

All our clothes in those days were made from natural fibres – wool, silk, cotton and linen. There was no nylon, terylene, elastane, polyester, and of course no blends like polycotton. The only man-made fabric we had was rayon – called artificial silk. If you went through your wardrobe and threw out all the clothes that did not have man-made fibres in them I don't think you'd have anything left.

The snag with natural fibres is that they have either to be dry-cleaned or laundered very carefully. Pure silk and cotton and linen creased easily and were very difficult to iron, especially with the irons we had then. Woollen jumpers shrink if they are washed in water that is too hot. Nowadays you can get woollens that are machine-washable, but it would not have been a lot of good in those days because there were no washing machines. Which is why Monday, washing day, was such an eventful day of the week.

CHAPTER 5

Irene

Before we tackle the washing, I must tell you a bit more about Irene, because, after my parents, she was the most important person in my life and I still think about her every time I put on a pair of socks. (She used to turn them inside out and then, magically, they came right-side out when I put them on.) I've told you that she brought us tea, cooked our meals, cleaned the doorstep, answered the door – and you may be wondering if she enjoyed life as much as we did. You might wonder even more when I tell you that she wore a uniform and had her main meals in the kitchen and not in the dining room with us, but that was the way things were done.

Being a maid was quite commonplace in those days. Fourteen was the school-leaving age, and hardly anyone stayed at school after that. Girls who lived in Norwich might get a job in a shop or factory, and country girls nearly always came into the city and worked as maids. City boys might start an apprenticeship or become office boys and work their way up, and most country boys would go to work on a farm. There was plenty for them to do because mechanisation had scarcely started.

Today the enormous tractors and combine harvesters have changed things so much that I know farms in Norfolk that used to employ 50 or 60 men even as late as the 1950s where now the only manpower is the farmer and his sons – and I expect you'll tell me that in Australia two or three men can run a farm that's measured, not in acres, but in square miles – or do I mean hectares and square kilometres? So there was plenty of work for country boys but in those days there was very little work for girls, and most of them would come into the city to work as maids.

It was a good job, and was pleasanter and better paid than working in a shop or a factory. A maid would have a comfortable room of her own (at home she might have to share with several sisters) and she had her uniform and all her meals provided. A job as a maid was so sought-after that, when my mother wanted a maid when she moved from London to Ipswich in 1923 (before I was born) so many girls applied for the job that she had to have a line of chairs both sides of the hall while they waited to be interviewed. She chose a girl called Lydia, who stayed with them for seven years, until they moved to Norwich.

When they moved, Lydia had enjoyed working for them so much that she came with them. But Norwich was 50 miles away from her family and she had never been so far away from them before, and she was homesick. So Lydia went back to Ipswich and my mother had to find a new maid. The Agency sent her a list of names, and she liked the sound of someone called Irene Howard. She was just setting off to visit her when there was a ring at the door. It was Irene, who had come with her mother to apply for the job. She got it on the spot.

Irene was 18 when she came to us, and she had already been working for another family in Norwich for four years. There were five children in that family, just as there are in yours, and they employed a cook and a housemaid as well as Irene, so she was at the bottom of the pile. When she came to us as a 'cook general' it was a big step up. (You might wonder what three servants found to do all day in a household the size of yours, but as you will see, there was a great deal more work in running a house in those days.)

Irene was a country girl with dark curly hair, rosy cheeks and a beautiful smile. (You can see how pretty she was from the photograph.) Years later when Irene was married and she and Stanley lived in the seaside town of Cromer her daughter Rosalind (she was called after my sister) entered a seaside beauty competition for a lark. She won – and went on to win lots more. I'm sure Irene would have won a beauty competition if there'd been any then.

Irene spoke with a Norfolk accent. (In those days country people spoke 'broad Norfolk' and were quite hard to understand.) There still is a Norfolk accent, but it isn't nearly so distinctive. But Norfolk people still say 'soup' instead of 'soap' – and, just to make things more confusing, 'soap' instead of 'soup'. And Norfolk choir-masters still have their work cut out to get their choristers to sing 'Holy, holy, holy' instead of 'Hooly, hooly, hooly.' Irene called a donkey a 'dicker', a floor cloth a 'dwile' and a heron a 'harnser'. She said her school mistress 'learnt' her (instead of 'taught' her). When she chatted with her friends they 'mardled.'

(Years later I learnt Anglo-Saxon and was delighted to discover that, when Beowulf spoke, he 'marthled' and 'lehren' means 'teach'. It just goes to show that Norfolk people see no reason to change their ways just because other people do.)

For her work in the morning Irene wore a blue cotton dress with a big white apron over it, and a white cap and black stockings and shoes (much the same as the uniform hospital nurses wore). In the afternoons she wore a brown dress with a fawn lace apron and a lace cap. Waitresses in tea shops dressed like that, too. She used to change after lunch, and I loved sitting on her bed chatting to her.

The best bit was when she showed me the things she had bought for her 'bottom drawer'. This really *was* a bottom drawer in her dressing table, and in it she put all sorts of things that would be useful for her home when she got married – things like sheets and pillowcases, towels and china. Her boy friend was Stanley Hudson, a tall young man with brown wavy hair, who worked for Laurence and Scott Electric Motors, and they were saving up to be married. In those days people didn't get married until they had some money saved up. Nobody, absolutely nobody, lived together before they were married. They waited for seven years.

I've tried to work out how much Irene was paid in today's values. I've found out since (nobody would have dreamed of telling me) that my father earned £1,000 a year before the war, which was a handsome salary in those days. This works out at £20 a week before tax. Irene was paid £1 a week which was hers to spend as she liked. I've read that today's equivalent of £1,000 is £160,000 = $348,000. If this is correct it would mean Irene was paid £8,000 a year = $18,500 a year. That's £150 or $355 a week.

(Talking about old money makes me realise how much I dislike decimalisation, and you must put up with me if I have a moan about it here. At the stroke of a pen the pounds shillings and pence I had grown up with disappeared, and so did our feet and inches. Can you imagine how maddening it is that I no longer even know what I weigh or how tall I am? And it's not just nostalgia that makes me dislike the metre. Feet and inches are measures made from man – my thumb is an inch, my foot is a foot, my pace is a yard – I'm a walking tape measure. But the metre doesn't relate to anything. I believe it's what the arrogant intellectuals of the French Revolution calculated – and calculated wrongly – was the millionth of the

circumference of the earth. Thank goodness horses are still measured in hands and in England you can still get a pint of beer! But enough complaining, I must get back to Irene.)

We kept in touch with Irene all her life, and used to go and see her right up until she died in 1994. I really believe my sisters and I meant almost as much to her as her own two daughters. One story that will show you what I mean is something that happened on the day of my father's funeral. There was a mix-up about the car that was to take Irene there, although it arrived eventually. She said: 'If that hadn't come, I'd have gone out on to the road and hitched a lift. I wasn't going to let my little Mrs Upjohn be on her own that day.' My sisters and I were there, plus a lot of friends and relations, but as far as Irene was concerned, my mother would have been on her own if she had not been there.

Another time, not long before she died, when Thelma and I were visiting her, we told her that our old house, Dorset House, was for sale. 'Let's buy it and go back and all live there together again,' she said.

Irene left us in August 1938 when she married her Stanley. Of course we all went to the wedding. I'd never been to a wedding before and didn't know what to expect.

At Christmas, my parents had taken us to London to see the pantomime at Drury Lane, and there was a breathtaking moment at the end when Cinderella and her prince had come down a staircase dressed in glorious glittering clothes. I thought Irene looked just as beautiful as she walked up the aisle on her father's arm to where Stanley, in his best suit, was waiting for her.

She was married at the little church at Caistor St Edmund and her two sisters, Agnes and Olive, were her bridesmaids. As we were all leaving, Irene suddenly turned and went over to another part of the churchyard, and I didn't understand why. She went to lay her bridal bouquet on her grandmother's grave.

So after that we had to find another maid. First there was Olive Johnson. We liked her a lot, but by this time I was at school all day and didn't spend so much time with her. When she left, another Olive, Olive Cutting, came to work for us. Her family lived near our seaside bungalow at Eccles. Then in about 1941 she had to register for war work and went off to a munitions factory. So that was the end of having a maid for us – and for everyone else as well.

I sometimes think that having a maid to look after me was very bad training – and that, if Irene had not been there to put away my toys and to pick my clothes up off the floor, I might perhaps have grown up a neat and tidy person. However, when I tiptoe through the chaos in your bedroom, Madison, I don't think that can be true.

CHAPTER 6

Put your Troubles through the Mangle

Monday is washing day. And it's washing day without a washing machine, a spin drier or tumble drier. As soon as breakfast has been cleared away, my mother and Irene set to work.

The coconut matting on the scullery floor is taken up, the clothes basket has been brought down from the bathroom and the clothes are tipped out and sorted. It's summer but, as soon as she got up, Irene lit the Ideal boiler that heats the water, and the scullery is boiling hot. There's a galvanised bucket of water heating on the gas stove in which the handkerchiefs will be boiled. Everyone in our house used handkerchiefs to blow their noses on – and they came in handy for mopping up spills and tying knots in to remember things as well. *(Do you know anyone who still owns a handkerchief, or do they all use tissues, like you?)*

Irene starts by filling the sink with hot water. The Ideal boiler does not have a thermostat and the water is almost boiling and comes out of the tap in spurts, so she has to be careful not to get scalded. Sometimes she uses washing powder – Oxydol, Rinso or Persil – and sometimes she uses a bar of Sunlight soap. The powders are soap powders, not detergents, and leave a lot of scum because Norwich water is very hard. So to make the water more alkaline, Irene adds washing soda, swishes it about. Then she puts a washboard in the sink and begins to rub the clothes up and down on it. *(A washboard is a flat piece of wood with a sheet of corrugated metal fixed on one side.)* Rubbing the clothes gets the dirt out of them, but it's very hard work – and hard on the clothes too.

If there are any extra-dirty marks – for instance on a shirt collar – she scrubs these with a small scrubbing brush. This means the collars wear out before the rest of the shirt, and the solution is to take the collar off and sew it back the other way up. A lot of shirts have separate collars, which get attached to the shirt by collar studs, front and back.

While Irene is rubbing the clothes up and down on the washboard, my mother is prodding the bucket of boiling handkerchiefs with a thick piece of wood she calls a 'copper stick'. *(A few years earlier she'd have been boiling my towelling nappies too. Disposable nappies hadn't been invented.)* The scullery is full of steam, and condensation is running

34

down the walls, which are painted in shiny cream paint. My mother and Irene are pink in the face and little tendrils of their hair are getting curly from the steam.

Irene starts the washing with 'the whites'. As she finishes washing small items she wrings them out and puts them on the enamel-topped scullery table. For big things like towels, she and my mother take an end each and twist it between them. Although they try to be careful, a lot of water slops on the floor. When the whites are finished Irene empties the sink and rinses the clothes in cold water, which makes her hands very red. There's Reckitt's Blue (a little cloth bag of blue dye, called a 'blue-bag') on a shelf above the sink and she dips this in the rinsing water and swishes it about to make the whites a better colour. She and my mother then wring the rest of the water out of the whites and put them into a galvanised bathtub.

While all this is going on I am riding my tricycle round the kitchen singing. My favourite song is one I have heard on the wireless:

Put your troubles through the mangle
Drive those blues away
Though the sun is shining
Through the window pane
When mother puts the washing out
It always rains
So put your troubles through the mangle
Like mother does on washing day

My mother and Irene each take a handle of the bathtub and carry it across the kitchen yard to the mangle in the outhouse opposite (next to the scary outside loo).

The mangle is a pair of wooden rollers mounted on an iron frame. There's an iron wheel at one side that moves the rollers as you turn it. You feed the wet clothes between the rollers and the water is squeezed out.

Irene turns the handle of the mangle while my mother feeds the folded clothes through the rollers. This has to be done carefully because if the buttons go through the wrong way they get broken, or are torn off. As the water is squeezed out, it pours into a bucket and a lot of it slops across the yard. Then they take dolly pegs and peg up the first batch of washing on the line. *(A dolly peg is a piece of wood with a round top that divides into a fork below. You trap the clothes between the fork and the clothes line to peg them up. If you paint a face on the knob and put a frill round it, it makes a very convincing doll.)* After hanging out the whites they sit down at the kitchen table for a cup of coffee. Instant coffee has not been invented and they use a teaspoonful of a thick brown liquid called Camp Coffee.

This comes in a tall square bottle with a picture of a British officer in the Indian Army sitting outside his tent. He wears a kilt, and his Indian servant, who wears a turban, stands beside him. I am given a cup of Ovaltine to fatten me up. *(I've just Googled Camp Coffee, Madison, - they still make it- and the label's just as I remember it!)*

After that they go back into the scullery and tackle 'the coloureds'. The woollen jumpers are the last to be washed, using Lux Flakes – little flakes of white soap. The jumpers have to be rinsed thoroughly to get out all the soap, mangled, and then put in the airing cupboard upstairs so they can dry flat. Some days it's raining and it's no use hanging anything up to dry outside. In spite of putting it through the mangle the washing is still very wet. *(Mangling does not get nearly as much water out of the clothes as a spin drier. That hasn't been invented yet – let alone a tumble drier.)*

There's a drying rack suspended from the scullery ceiling and the clothes have to be dried on that. *(You may have seen these in craft shops. They put bunches of dried flowers on them these days.)* My mother lowers the rack and she and Irene arrange the clothes on it. Then she pulls it up and fixes the rope on a cleat. The clothes take a lot longer to dry indoors, but they do get dry eventually. However they often smell of whatever has been cooked underneath them – kippers sometimes.

It's now getting on for half past twelve and the rest of the family will be home soon, expecting a meal on the table. Irene mops up the scullery floor, which is soaking wet. Then she peels the potatoes and puts them on to cook and opens a tin of peas. My mother cuts up the remains of the Sunday joint and lays it out on a meat dish. She empties a big tin of peaches into a serving dish. Irene makes some custard, and then goes into the dining room to lay the table. My mother goes upstairs to tidy up. She puts on lots of hand cream to try to stop her hands getting red.

When lunch has been cleared away and washed up there's still some work to do. The dinner napkins from the dining room, and the doilies, the lace-edged table cloths, napkins and embroidered tray cloths we use for posh tea have to be starched to make them crisp. *(This is how it's done. You put a tablespoonful of starch – a white powder that looks a bit like flour – in a basin and pour boiling water over it. This makes it go thick and shiny. You put this stuff in an enamel bowl and add cold water until you've got a milky liquid. Then you dip the damp things in it and swish them about before taking them out to the shed to mangle them again.)* If you saved all the washing in your house to be done on just one day there would be the most horrendous amount and, even though ours was for just five people not seven as in your family, you must be wondering how it could all be done in the time. There are two reasons for this – the first is that we made our clothes last longer between washes, whereas you seem to wash everything, even if it has only been worn once and whether it looks dirty or not. The second reason is that not everything was washed at home – a lot of things were sent to the Wensum Laundry.

Before the days of washing machines there were lots of commercial laundries because washing things by hand – especially large items – was such a hassle. The stuff sheets were made of was much thicker and heavier than it is today. Just imagine putting a double sheet in the sink and bashing it up and down, hoping to get it clean. And after that you have to wring it, mangle it, hope to get it dry and, finally, iron it. One sheet per bed is washed each week. *(The bottom sheet is washed and the top sheet moves to the bottom.)* So in our house there's one double sheet and four single sheets to be washed every week. That's such a lot of work that the sheets are sent to the laundry, plus the big white dining room cloths and some of my father's shirts. *(The laundry sews a little mark to show who they belong to. In old detective stories you'll find that unidentified corpses have always had the laundry marks cut out of their clothes.)*

In winter, when it's cold and wet in England and it's hard to get washing dry, my mother sends towels, pillowcases and lots of other things, too.

Luckily for us, today has been fine and the washing has dried. My mother and Irene have taken it in and folded it. Tomorrow is Tuesday – ironing day.

CHAPTER 7

All in a Day's Work

Tuesday may be ironing day, but that's a job for the afternoon, and the morning's work has to be done first. After breakfast Irene clears away and washes up by hand. There are no dishwashers. She washes the dishes in Oxydol, or swishes bits of soap in a little wire cage in the water, because there are no dishwashing liquids. Then she rinses the plates, stacks them on the draining board and dries them. There is a big wooden plate rack fixed to the scullery wall but we don't use it to drain the plates because my mother says it gets slimy and is impossible to clean – which is true.

Now it's time to make the beds, which we 'turn back to air' when we get up. My mother usually gives a hand with the beds because – though the people who live in faraway Sweden and Switzerland might have them – nobody in England has a duvet, so it is a two-man job. They tuck the top and bottom sheets in tightly (fitted sheets have not been invented) then tuck in two or three blankets – and then arrange a bedspread and an eiderdown on top.

The dining room is dusted every day and Irene polishes the table and vacuums the floor with a cleaner called The Goblin – it's very noisy and looks a bit like a carpet sweeper, with a bag attached that collects all the dust.

Sometimes one of the downstairs rooms is 'turned out'. All the furniture is put in the middle of the room and everything cleaned and polished. Fitted carpets have not been invented and each room has a square carpet in the centre with linoleum filling in the spaces round the edges. Ours is patterned to look like wood-block flooring. Irene polishes this on her hands and knees. One of my best games is to ride on her back and pretend she is a horse. One day I overbalance and land face-down in a tin of floor polish – which has a very sharp edge. When they pick me up my face is covered in polish with blood oozing through it. Everyone is screaming. I am bawling. Irene rushes off to fetch a doctor who lives nearby. By the time he arrives the polish has been cleaned off and they can see that my eye has not been damaged which is what all the fuss was about. He calms everyone down and says there is no need for stitches and there will not be a scar. *(He is wrong. I still have the scar today.)* In spite of the commotion, they still manage to get midday dinner on the table in time. After it has been cooked, eaten and cleared away, and she has changed into her afternoon uniform, on Tuesday Irene and I do the ironing.

Irene spreads an ironing blanket on the kitchen table and puts an old sheet on top. (We've got a wooden ironing board, but she doesn't like using it.) There's an extra light socket hanging beside the light over the table, and Irene plugs the iron into that. It doesn't have an earth, and sparks fly out sometimes. I get out my toy iron and sit next to her.

There's a great heap of clothes on the kitchen dresser. Everything gets ironed – vests, knickers, pyjamas, shirts, pillowcases, handkerchiefs, tray cloths, table cloths, doilies, cotton dresses – socks, even. Irene irons the things first and then gives them to me to finish off.

Unlike modern irons, the electric iron does not have a thermostat and just keeps getting hotter and hotter. Irene has to keep switching off and on again. It's hard to judge the correct heat, and Irene uses an old piece of sheet to test the iron to see whether it is too hot and will leave scorch marks. Ironing my mother's silk petticoat is particularly dicey.

(Even so, it's a lot less problematic than with the irons my mother used to use. These were 'flat irons' made of solid iron and you heated them on a sheet of metal over the gas jet on the cooker. We've still got them, but they stay in the kitchen cupboard these days.)

Steam irons have not been invented so, if the clothes are too dry to iron, Irene sprinkles them with water and then rolls them up so the moisture spreads more evenly. Things that have been starched are particularly tricky because, if the iron is too hot, the starch sticks to the iron and makes a brown film that has to be scratched off with a knife. As we finish each piece, anything still damp is hung on a wooden clothes horse, or over the nursery fireguard, or put in the airing cupboard.

Every afternoon has its own special job. On Wednesdays Irene and I clean the silver and brass. The kitchen table is covered with newspaper and Irene tips the silver polish into a big spoon for her and a little spoon for me and we get out some old rags – some of our old cotton knickers, usually. *(Your cutlery is stainless steel, Madison, which never needs cleaning, but ours is made from silver or silver plate, which tarnishes.)* We also have a lot of brass and silver things, some useful, some ornamental. As well as the spoons and forks there's the silver teapot and hot water jug, the silver candlesticks and biscuit barrel, and little silver jam dishes. Then there's the copper coal scuttle, brass fire irons and toasting fork and the copper pots on the kitchen mantelpiece. All these have to be cleaned every week. It's fun seeing them come up all nice and shiny – and afterwards we have tea and little biscuits with pink sugar icing on top.

Thursday afternoon is Irene's afternoon off, when she goes out with her boyfriend Stanley.

They sometimes go to cinema. My sisters and I sometimes go to the cinema with my mother – we call it 'going to the pictures'. They take me to see a Laurel and Hardy film, which is meant to be funny because they fall off a boat into the water. I think they are going to drown and crouch under the seat, sobbing. They also take me to see a Shirley Temple film in which her parents are knocked down by a car, and a cake with an aeroplane on it lies smashed in the middle of the road. I sob under the seat again, and they don't take me any more. (I think your nerves must be a lot stronger nowadays, Madison. If I had watched some of the films that your little sister Zoe, who is seven, watches without a tremor, I should have ended up having nightmares for weeks – though there was a moment in the last Harry Potter where she had to be taken out.)

Friday is baking day. Irene and I make a big fruit cake, a Victoria sponge – which is cut in half when it's cold and filled with cream and jam – lots of little fruit cakes (called rock cakes) and some biscuits. I butter the baking tins while Irene beats the margarine and sugar together with a wooden spoon until they are creamy. (The margarine is a hard block, not the soft margarine you have in plastic tubs these days.) There are no food processors, and this is very hard work. If we make meringues, whisking whites of eggs takes ages because we don't even have a hand beater – only a fork to whisk with.

A bright fire is burning, the Triplex oven is getting hot, and soon there's a lovely smell of baking. Sometimes we burn the cakes slightly

40

because the oven has got too hot, but they're always delicious. Even so, the bit I like best is scraping the mixing bowls.

When the cakes are cooling on a cake rack we put all the ingredients away in the larder. There were no kitchen units in our kitchen, as there are today. The china is kept in the china pantry, the saucepans on shelves in the scullery and the food in the larder. The larder is a very large walk-in cupboard, like a small room, with a high window. Originally it just had a set of deep shelves on each side. My father has had these taken out and had two tall metal cabinets made, with perforated metal doors. Before that, my mother tells me, the mice frisked about on the shelves and nibbled the food.

(Yes, we did have mice in our house and my parents set mouse traps for them. I took biscuits to school to eat at break time and sometimes left some in my raincoat pocket. The mice found them, and chewed a hole in the pocket to get at them.)

We put away the flour (which lives in a big enamel bin marked **FLOUR**), the sugar, the sultanas, the butter and margarine, the eggs, the milk and the cream. Nothing goes in the refrigerator, because we haven't got one. No one else in West Parade has either, though the Bostons have an ice cabinet, which is an insulated wooden cupboard which is kept cold with ice they get from the fishmonger. *(Not having a refrigerator isn't as inconvenient in England as it is in Australia, because England has a colder climate. But there weren't refrigerators in Australia in those days, either – though I've seen ice cabinets, like the Bostons' in the Powerhouse Museum in Sydney.)*

The ingredients we use to make the cakes have not been bought in a supermarket – there aren't any supermarkets. They have been delivered by George, with his horse and cart.

CHAPTER 8

Half a Pound of Tuppenny Rice

George worked for Mr Bassingthwaite who had a shop in Nelson Street nearby. My mother telephoned her order every week and George delivered it on Wednesday afternoons.

We were one of the few people who had a telephone. It was a wooden box fixed to the wall in the hall. It had a speaker in the centre and a receiver hanging on a hook at the side. When you lifted the receiver, you turned the handle at the side and the line connected to the Telephone Exchange and a telephonist asked: 'Number, Please.' You told her (it was usually a woman in daytime and a man in the evenings) which number you wanted and she replied 'Putting you through.' Then she would plug your line into a socket on a complicated switchboard. Telephonists were trained to speak very distinctly, and my mother would also put on a special voice when she answered the telephone.

(I'm still amazed that telephone calls now bounce off a satellite –and by your mobile phone can send text messages, record calls, play music, take photographs and make video recordings – I'm still getting to grips with my very simple one.)

We never made international calls (we didn't know anyone who lived abroad) but they were horrendously expensive. Even a 'trunk' call to London cost a lot. My mother once accidentally ran up a big bill chatting to one of her sisters. *(I believe you've done the same sort of thing, Madison, on your mobile phone when you were younger.)*

Because George delivered our groceries we hardly ever went to Mr Bassingthwaite's little shop, but it was nothing like the enormous supermarkets you are used to. There was no question of wandering round and taking things off the shelves. A big wooden counter, with a set of shining brass scales on it, stood near the back of the shop. The shop assistant, who wore a brown cotton overall, stood behind it. You asked for whatever it was you wanted and he (it was usually a man) went to the shelf and brought it back to the counter. Things like tins of Heinz Baked Beans and bottles of Camp Coffee were easy, but what made shopping more complicated was the fact that hardly anything was pre-packed but was measured out as it was needed. Weighing tea was quite a performance. First Mr Bassingthwaite used the brass scales to weigh out a quarter of a pound. Then he took a special piece of paper and banged it with a ruler to make creases in it. He poured the tea onto the paper, which he folded into an oblong shape. He then reached up and pulled a length of string out of a container hanging from the ceiling, and tied the tea up into a neat packet. It was done very quickly, and the packet looked perfect.

Tea bags had not been invented. We never made tea in a cup and the only tea variety was Indian. When we got home we tipped the packet of tea into a tea caddy. When we made tea we spooned it into the silver pot, warming the pot first.

The sugar came in sacks, and was weighed on the scales and then scooped into thick blue paper bags. The rice and tapioca and semolina for those awful puddings were weighed into bags while we waited, too. The cheese was cut off big blocks, using a piece of wire – the way they still do it in expensive delis nowadays.

The bacon wasn't ready-sliced. Mr Bassingthwaite would put what looked like half a pig onto a big red machine and whizz it up and down – zing, zing – towards a circular knife to cut it into rashers. You could choose how thickly it was cut.

Because nothing was pre-packed, the shop had a wonderful smell. It was compounded of spices and tea and coffee and bacon – and lots of other aromas I can't identify.

We never took our shopping away with us. On Wednesdays George would drive his horse and cart to the top of West Parade and stop outside our front gate. Then he carried the boxes round to the back door. He would not have dreamed of going to the front door – only visitors called there. Everyone else used the back door – the Tradesmen's Entrance. His horse stayed outside the front gate with a nosebag – which is a small sack of food.

It stayed there for quite a long time, because George was always asked into the kitchen for a cup of tea. He wore breeches, leather leggings, a driving coat of khaki cotton and a pork pie hat, which he took off when he came into the house. *(This is a brown felt hat with a brim. It has a ridge round the edge of the crown and a slight dome in the middle of it, rather the same shape as a pork pie.)*

George had bright blue eyes, a round brown face and a gingery moustache with pointed ends. He used to say he had worked with horses all his life. I seem to remember there was usually some straw on the floor after he left.

George brought Monkey Brand hearthstone for the front doorsteps, bars of Sunlight soap for washing day and Mansion Polish for the floors and the dining room table. He also used to bring Caley's Ginger Beer and Whiteways Cydrax for us, and bottles of Steward & Patterson beer for my father. These had a thick screw-in stopper and were packed in a sort of wigwam of straw to stop them breaking. When George brought the blue paper bags of rice and sultanas and tapioca, I used to help my mother put them into glass storage jars.

After George and his horse had left, one of our neighbours, a retired schoolteacher called Mr Looker, would rush out of his house with a bucket and shovel and collect the droppings George's horse had deposited, to put on his roses. My mother thought this was not a proper thing to do.

Meat, fish and bread were delivered, too, but they didn't arrive by horse and cart. An errand boy from the butcher and another from the fishmonger would call every morning riding their bicycles, which had very big baskets on the front. *(Errand boys in those days always seemed to be very cheerful and they whistled as they rode along. I don't hear anybody whistling songs nowadays. I suppose they are listening to their iPods instead.)* My mother gave them her order, and they would come back and deliver it in time for it to be cooked for our midday meal.

Because there weren't any domestic refrigerators, people had to shop for perishable food a day at a time. I can't remember how the vegetables arrived, but I expect the greengrocer sent a boy round, too. Vegetables were seasonal – you could not buy all of them all the year round. Peas and spring greens came in the spring and parsnips and Brussels sprouts (ugh!) in winter.

Milk was delivered every day. In my Norfolk village it still is. My first memory is of milk being delivered by motor van in one-pint glass bottles, but my sister Thelma remembers the milkman driving his horse and cart up West Parade, dipping a pint measure into a churn full of milk, and then filling up the jugs the maids brought out to him. *(Mr Looker got another opportunity to dash out with his shovel, I expect.)*

Bread was delivered every day, too. The high window in the larder was always left open. My mother would leave a note saying 'One brown, two white' and the errand boy would pop it through onto the window sill.

There were lots of small shops near West Parade, most of them owned by the people who ran them. But when you went 'down the city' as we called it, into the centre of Norwich, the same thing was true. The big shop on the corner of the market place, Jarrolds, was owned and run by the Jarrold family. It still is. There was Stevenson's Sports Shop and Pilch's Sports Shop, Bushell's Umbrella Shop, Curl's Department store, Butcher's Drapers, Ridley's Outfitters, Bonds Department Store, Deacon's Fish Restaurant, Garlands Drapers, Cowell's the Seedsman, Copeman's grocery, Buckingham's Shoe Shop, Levine's Jewellers – all owned by people we knew, and some of whose daughters I went to school with later on.

Apart from Woolworth's and Marks & Spencers, the only chain shops I remember in Norwich then were Boots the Chemist, Mac Fisheries and Sainsbury's. Sainsbury's is now a huge supermarket chain in England, but the Norwich shop in those days was quite a small place, with tiled walls, on Gentleman's Walk opposite the market. Uniformed shop assistants cut off the amount of cheese and butter you needed – and you had to go to a separate part of the shop to pay for your purchases.

In those days the price of groceries was always the same no matter in which shop you bought them – and most of the goods had the price printed on the label. There were no 'Specials' or bargain offers. But then a change in the law meant the retailer could sell below the 'recommended' price, and so the big shops could afford to reduce their profit to increase their sales. But small shops, like Mr Bassingthwaite's, needed to charge the full price – and so they soon went out of business.

Virtually all the big shops, too, in Norwich, which used to be privately-owned have either gone out of business or been taken over by huge organisations. So now, no matter which town or city in England you go to, you find the same shops along the high street. In fact, you even find the same no matter which country you are in. You can shop at Monsoon, Laura Ashley or the Body Shop whether you are in England or Australia – and you can have coffee at Starbucks and eat at McDonalds or KFC all over the world.

The shops were open only from 9am to 5.30pm Monday to Saturday. They also shut one afternoon a week for Early Closing. This was to give the people who worked there a half day off. Nobody, except factories, employed shift workers as they do today.

45

(Once when I was shopping in your local Woolworth's I saw a notice apologising to customers because it was closing at 10pm instead of midnight. And a lot of supermarkets in England – and Australia – are now open 24 hours a day. I suppose someone must shop at three in the morning.)

The English Woolworth's is not the same as the huge supermarket chain in Australia. In those days it was called the Threepence and Sixpenny Store – you could buy anything there for 3d and 6d. Years later it became a cut-price department store, and now – unthinkable as it would have been back then – it has gone bankrupt and no longer exists. (Although I believe it's been reinvented on line.)

When I was so small I could scarcely see over the counters, I loved going to Woolworths with my mother. Sometimes she would buy me a necklace of graduated 'pearls', which came in a blue plush case that fastened with a catch, or a bottle of Parma Violet scent, which I would take home and pour all over my hair.

Woolworths had beautiful polished wood floors (you notice the floors when you're small, you're so close to them) and one day I was amazed to see the elegant Mrs Boswell's older son Graham sweeping them. When I asked my mother what he was doing, she explained he was going in for management, and people had to start at the bottom. (I don't know whether people still do this, but I think it's a good principle. It's all very well arriving with an MBA, but when you're sweeping the floor you learn a lot of things about the way things work that degree courses don't teach you.)

After we'd been to Woolworth's it was often time for my mother to join her friends for a cup of coffee in one of the big department stores.

CHAPTER 9

Coffee & Kings

My favourite place to go for coffee was Jarrolds, where we went up to the top floor in a lift. We knew the lift was coming down for us because, through the wire cage, we could see the big weight that counter-balanced it going up. We didn't step in and press a button as you do, Madison. There was a lift attendant who sat on a stool, and whose job it was to turn a brass handle to get to the correct floor. He then opened the two sets of folding lattice metal doors to let us out. At each floor he would call out the goods you could buy there. (He only had one arm and my mother said he had been wounded in the war – the 1914-18 war, that is.)

Norwich market place, seen from Jarrolds corner. The picture shows it, with the trams, a few years before we moved to Norwich.
Later on the success of my father's buses put the trams out of business.

In Jarrolds restaurant we sat at tables with white cloths, and coffee came in a 'silver' metal coffee pot with a matching jug of hot milk. (I guess the coffee was made by pouring boiling water on to ground coffee.) Coffee machines had not been invented and when you asked for 'coffee' this is what arrived. Today if you ask for coffee, you're asked 'What sort?' The beans can be Brazilian, or Mexican or Columbian – and you can have long black, short black, espresso, cappuccino, latte, skinny latte – and all of them can be large, medium or small – and what's more they can also be decaf. I'm not complaining. The coffee nowadays is absolutely delicious – and it's even better in Australia than in England.

In the middle of Jarrolds restaurant there was a railed-off area with potted palms, and while my mother and her friends were drinking coffee, a pianist and two violinists would be playing. This was the only way to provide music because there were no loudspeakers or PA systems. If you wanted music it had to be live.

(Something I dislike about shopping today, Madison, is the constant blare of piped music in shops and supermarkets. Usually it's so meaningless that I can ignore it, but when they start belting out jazzed up versions of Christmas carols and Jingle Bells from October onwards, it's as much as I can do not to run screaming out into the street.)

Grown-ups don't seem to realise that children can overhear them, and, even better than the ice cream they used to buy me, I loved listening to their conversations. When they discussed hats I was puzzled to hear they thought one was 'chick', because it didn't have any feathers. *(Years later I found they meant 'chic', which is pronounced 'sheek'.)* But far more interesting than the clothes chat was all the talk about the Prince of Wales' affair with Mrs Simpson.

The English newspapers kept quiet about it *(something else that has changed – it would be all over the tabloids now)* but the foreign press was not so discreet and everyone knew – or guessed – what was going on. My mother and her friends were outraged. It was an affront to the standards they lived by and which they took such pains to uphold.

To understand the reaction you must bear in mind that practically nobody was divorced at that time – except for a few film stars and the like. Getting a divorce was very difficult and very expensive – and was regarded as a great social stigma. For instance, divorcees were not allowed in the Royal Enclosure at Ascot. (I expect they've changed that rule now that Prince Charles, Princess Anne and Prince Andrew are all divorced.) We weren't likely to be invited to Ascot but, nearer home in Norwich, none of my friends' parents were divorced and I didn't know anyone who was.

(So many people are now divorced that a schoolteacher friend of mine told me recently that, if she had to send a note about Bill Smith to his home, she could not address it to 'Mr & Mrs Smith' or even 'Mrs Smith' or 'Mr Smith'. She had to write 'To the person in charge of Bill Smith'.)

There was a song at the time that the errand boys sang:

Who's that going down the street
Mrs Simpson, ain't she sweet
She's had husbands three or four
Now she's knocked on Edward's door

The thought that the heir to the throne was 'entangled' or 'ensnared' by an American woman who had not only divorced one husband but was still married to her second was horrifying. Although Queen Elizabeth is still Queen of Australia, I don't suppose she means a great deal to you and your contemporaries (though you might have seen the film The Queen) and you will find it hard to understand what very great admiration, affection and respect everyone in England had for the royal family at that time. The situation became critical when the Prince of Wales' father George V died in January 1936. The moment that happened, Edward was proclaimed King Edward VIII. All the arrangements were completed for his coronation on 12th May 1937, fifteen months later. Even the Coronation mugs were on sale.

(The unfortunate shopkeepers who had bought them must have been hard put to give them away later, but they're collectors' items now. You know I'm mad about commemorative mugs, Madison. I've got one.)

What was to become of Mrs Simpson? The prospect of a twice-divorced American being crowned Queen of England was absolutely unthinkable. My mother and her friends agreed it could not be allowed to happen. So did the Prime Minister, Stanley Baldwin and the Archbishop of Canterbury. We knew nothing of the negotiations that went on behind the scenes. The first we knew was the announcement that King Edward had decided he would abdicate – which meant he would give up the throne and that his younger brother would be king in his place. So we had a coronation after all and I got my first coronation mug. I remember listening to the King's abdication broadcast, and my parents' reaction of shock and sorrow – tinged with relief. With hindsight, how fortunate we were.

My mother usually had coffee in a restaurant on the top floor of one of the big shops (Curls and Buntings as well as Jarrolds). She never went to a café with chairs outside on the pavement. There weren't any. One of the things we were told about the French was that they had the strange habit of putting tables and chairs outside their restaurants and eating out there in the street.

No one I knew had ever been to France. Crossing the Channel was adventurous and expensive. It meant catching the boat train to Dover from Victoria and then spending several hours at sea. Now you can get a train in London and be in the centre of Paris in two hours – and it doesn't cost a lot.

We never ate outside in the street in England. It had nothing to do with the weather – it's much the same in England as it is in France – it just was not done. There are plenty of outdoor cafés in England now, of course, and in Australia there are so many of them that I wonder there are enough customers to fill them, but they all seem to flourish. After coffee my mother would sometimes go to Garlands, near Jarrolds in London Street, to try on hats.

My mother and her friends always wore hats and gloves, winter and summer, when they went down the city. But it wasn't just the stuffy English who dressed like that. If you look at Max du Pain's photographs of Sydney in the 1930s you'll see virtually everyone – men and women – wearing hats. And fashion photographs show that hats were an integral part of the outfit – and very smart they look. Nowadays a hat seems to have become some sort of fancy dress, worn only at weddings and – for some reason – watching horse-racing.

When we went to Garlands, the first person we saw was the 'shop walker'. He was an elegant, grey-haired man who wore striped trousers and a black jacket. His job was to wander about the shop, to welcome customers, to draw their attention to any special promotion, and to direct them to whichever department they wanted. As we went to 'Hats' we would often meet a beautiful young woman with pale blonde hair who was called 'the mannequin'. Her job was to walk about the shop dressed in various outfits to display them to the customers. You could stop her, and she would explain about the clothes and tell you where to get them and what they cost. *(I thought this was a job I should like once I was grown up.)*

The hats were kept in deep drawers, sorted by colour. When my mother bought one, she sometimes paid in cash. There were no tills on the counter, and shop assistants didn't handle the money. The salesgirl would put the cash into a cylinder which she twisted to make it close. She then put the cylinder into a compartment with a flap, which shut with a whoosh, and it would go whizzing away to the accounts department somewhere in the building. A few minutes later it would come back and land with a thump, with the change and a receipt inside it.

When we went shopping in Butcher's Drapery Shop, the system was slightly different. The salesgirl put the money in a container and then pulled a trigger to send it whizzing along an overhead wire to where the cashier sat, like a spider in a web, at the centre of the shop.

(It's very different today when the till automatically records the price, the amount tendered and the change due. It can have its disadvantages, though. I know a boy doing a Saturday job who, when the electricity went off, couldn't work out how much change to give a customer who gave him $20 for a $2.75 purchase.

There were no bar codes either. I'm always amazed that the till and weighing scales can give me a receipt for 'Onions brown .378 kg at 2.48/kg = 0.94 just from scanning a few black lines. And of course there were no debit or credit cards.)

But if you didn't happen to have enough money in your purse, you could always pay by cheque. The disadvantage was that, if you did, you were not allowed to take the goods away with you. The shop would deliver them in three days time, once the cheque had been cleared.

My mother had an account at several of the shops, which meant you could take things away at once, and they sent a bill at the end of the month. It also meant that, if you couldn't make up your mind which dress you wanted, you could take one or two 'on approval' to try on at home, and bring back those you did not want – or all of them – a few days later.

(This might seem very trusting, but it isn't much different today when you can get a refund on goods you've bought provided you have the receipt. In those days shops were very difficult about giving refunds, and most of them would only grudgingly take things back and give you credit.)

The only item you were not allowed to take 'on approval' was a hat. I suppose the shop thought you might wear it for a special occasion and then take it back. But hats were for all occasions, not just special ones. And wearing a hat had another advantage, apart from looking smart. It meant it didn't matter too much what your hair looked like underneath it.

CHAPTER 10

Making Waves

Almost every day was a bad hair day when I was a child. I've told you about the once-weekly bath night – and that's when most people would wash their hair, too.

Amami was the only shampoo there was, as far as I know, and a lot of people just used ordinary soap – and there were no conditioners, no heated rollers or electric tongs. (*When I went to a party my mother would sometimes curl my hair by heating curling tongs in the gas flame of the cooker. If the tongs were too hot, your hair got singed and broke off.*) And there were no hair-driers, apart from the ones at the hairdressers.

Not having a hair-drier would not be so disastrous today because so many people often just have a shower and leave their hair to get dry naturally. But in those days no grown woman would ever have gone out with her hair long and loose, or pulled back in a pony tail. And not many people wore their hair short and straight. Hairstyles were complicated and hard to maintain. My mother and most of her friends had a 'Marcel wave' and a tight sausage of curl at the back of their heads and curls in front. This was quite hard to achieve. Unless your hair was naturally curly, you first had to have a 'permanent wave' which meant a visit to the hairdresser, where your hair was rolled up and attached by electric wires to something hanging from the ceiling that looked a bit like a chandelier. It cost a lot, and often your hair went frizzy afterwards.

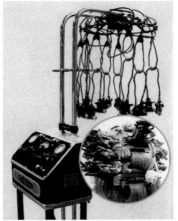

When my mother washed her hair at home, she would roll it up in curlers and hair pins and then put a scarf over it until it was dry, or sometimes she would lie down near the fire to help it dry quicker. At night she would put her hair in curlers and over this she would put a 'sleeping cap' which was made of pink net and had ribbons that tied under her chin. It must have been very lumpy to sleep on. (I wonder if she ever regretted the days when her hairstyle was easy to look after – long hair pulled back into a bun. I'm sure my father must have done!)

But in his own way my father was a fashion victim too, because until Gillette invented the safety razor in 1904 most men had beards - like my grandfather – and didn't have the chore of shaving every day.

My mother had had her long hair cut off before I was born, in the 1920s when short hair became fashionable. *(She kept it and when the New Look made long hair fashionable after the war, I made it into a bun, which I attached with hair pins.)*

Short skirts had come into fashion at the same time as short hair. And even though they were below the knee – not thigh-high like today – my mother must have felt very daring when she first wore them. You have to remember that, when she was a child, she would have been shocked if *her* mother's skirt had been short enough to show her *ankles*.

There was only one hair style for men – 'short back and sides'. It would have been unthinkable for any man to have long hair – let alone a pony tail. The only sort of a man who might have had an earring or a tattoo would have been some disreputable old sailor. A lot of men used to put Brylcreem on their hair, which made it shiny and kept it tidy. (My father didn't but he didn't have much hair.) This left marks on the backs of armchairs when they leaned their heads back. However, it was not as bad as the macassar oil men used before Brylcreem was invented. This left greasy marks on the upholstery, which were difficult to get off. So some people used to put pieces of cloth over the backs of armchairs – just as they do on airline seats today – which were called 'antimacassars'. *(My mother thought these were dreadfully old-fashioned. She put them in the same category as aspidistras – an evergreen plant old-fashioned people used to keep in their 'front room'.)*

A lot more people had grey hair. The colours that hairdressers used looked harsh and unnatural – bright yellow, dark brown, inky black, fierce auburn, and vivid ginger. It was frowned on to dye your hair, and everyone could see at a glance that you did. *(I think it must have been about the 1960s that hair dyes changed. I remember an advertisement: 'Does she, doesn't she? Hair colour so natural only her hairdresser knows for sure.')* After that lots more people didn't go grey any more. Later on hair colours changed again, with streaks and highlights. And it was years before coloured hair – pink and blue and green became something to flaunt. *(I love the highlights and wild colours. And I can almost persuade myself I've turned into a natural blonde as I've got older.)*

Make-up was primitive too, and a lot of women didn't wear any – and if you did it had to be 'discreet'. There were no coloured foundation creams and there were no blushers – just 'rouge', a bright red powder which could make you look like a clown if you weren't careful. My mother used Ponds Vanishing Cream and pink face powder which she kept in a glass pot on her dressing table and dabbed on with a swansdown powder puff. Her lipstick was a dark red called 'Tabu'. There were no pale shades. She never wore coloured nail polish. Very few people did. I only knew one person who wore eye make-up – our neighbour Daisy Nokes.

Daisy Nokes lived two doors away. She had bright yellow dyed hair and bright blue eye shadow, which was considered very 'fast'. She had worked as a dresser at the Theatre Royal – which perhaps is where she picked up the idea. She used to keep house for her father who wore a broad-brimmed hat and a cape, and twirled a walking stick as he walked down West Parade.

Talking about Daisy Nokes reminds me about something I should have said when I was writing about our neighbours. All the houses in West Parade were occupied by families in various combinations. As well as Daisy Nokes and her father, there were two more households of a widower and his grown-up daughter living together. One of them was Mr Beattie, who had had a stroke and used to walk slowly up and down West Parade leaning on his walking stick every day. He was the only person I ever saw taking exercise for its own sake.

Then there were five families like ours, with school-age children; six families with grown-up children who were out at work; three households with brother and sister living together; three with widowed mothers and their grown-up children; and several sets of retired couples. Because in those days children didn't leave home until they got married.

The fact that families stayed together is the reason for another big difference. Nowadays there are so many retirement villages and old people's homes that you may find this hard to believe, but when I was a child, there were no retirement villages, old people's homes, or even sheltered accommodation. Unless they were very ill and had to go into hospital, old people were looked after at home by their own families. And also, as you'll see, people didn't live as long in those days.

But sometimes, because of their work, unmarried sons did move away from their families – and this brings me to the subject of lodgers. Nowadays men can easily manage to cook and clean for themselves. But in those days keeping a house clean and cooking meals were both so complicated that a man would not contemplate doing it himself. Instead he would become a 'lodger' and live as a member of another family, and pay them every week for his 'board and lodging'.

One or two families in West Parade had lodgers – and lodgers are very important in our family history. Because if it weren't for my grandmother taking in lodgers, I shouldn't be here – and that means you wouldn't be, either.

Your great-great-grandparents and their children in 1899

CHAPTER 11

Such a Nice Young Man

We'll have to take a look at that Victorian photograph to explain why my grandmother took in lodgers. It was taken in 1899 when she was thirty-six years old and, as you can see, she had seven children. She had an eighth child a year after the photograph was taken. Eight children might seem a large family, but they were just the ones that survived. She told my mother she'd had fourteen children – one for every year of her marriage.

Losing six children as babies might seem horrendous to you, but it was not unusual in those days. Even when I was growing up in the 1930s I heard an old country woman telling my mother, 'I've had eight and buried four' as if it were nothing out of the ordinary.

But things were to get worse for Sarah, because soon after her eighth surviving child was born, my grandfather died. He was only thirty-nine. There was no Social Security in those days and very few people, if any, had life insurance. Then, a few years later, her eldest son Arthur died too. He was 17, and was the only member of the family earning money.

So there she was, with a family to support and no money coming in. But she had a large house – and she was used to looking after a family. So she took in lodgers in order to pay her way.

Quite a few years later, one of them was a young engineer called Wilfred Upjohn. He had come back from Canada where he'd worked on the Canadian Pacific Railway. Now he was helping to design the first motor buses.

A man called Thomas Tilling had started a bus company back in 1846, but of course in those days the buses, like all other vehicles were horse-drawn.

(Did you know that in 1900 there were so many horses in London they deposited 1,000 tons of horse muck every day?)

© *TfL London Transport Museum*

56

Horses had been the means of transport for centuries and people were slow to believe that the newfangled motor cars could ever replace them. The breakthrough came in 1896, which was the year my father left school and started his apprenticeship with steam engines. Because this was the year the Red Flag Law was repealed.

You might find this hard to believe, but until then motor cars were thought to be so dangerous that they were only allowed on the road if there was a man with a red flag walking in front of them to warn people to get out of the way. Clearly motor cars were not going to replace horses while they could only go at walking speed. But once the Red Flag Law was repealed, the Thomas Tilling Company, now run by his sons, decided to experiment and see if they could replace their horse buses with motor buses.

I found plenty of photographs of early motor buses when I looked on line, and the earliest I could find were taken in 1911 and 1913. But then I remembered this photograph of my father, which had been tucked away in a cupboard at Dorset House. It shows him, with a group of colleagues, seated in front of an early Tilling motor bus (he's in the middle of the front row). I guess the old man on the right is Richard Tilling and the two lads on the left are his schoolboy sons.

This photograph was taken in 1904. And I realised that this must be the first-ever London double-decker motor bus. No wonder they all turned out for the photograph, including the bus driver.

The engineering problems my father and his colleagues solved were formidable. First of all a metal chassis had to be designed, since the wooden framework of the horse bus was too flimsy to support the heavy petrol engine. *(In the Power House Museum in Sydney I've seen an early motor car in which the frame of the bodywork is made of wood – just like a horse-drawn carriage.)*

Then the thin iron-bound wooden wheels of the horse bus had to be replaced by metal wheels with rubber tyres (the ones in the photograph are solid, not pneumatic).

The result was heavy, but weight was no longer a drawback with the power of 24 notional horses – not two flesh and blood ones – to pull the bus and its thirty-four passengers. Then there was the problem of training the bus drivers.

The old drivers were horsemen and had no idea how to drive a motor vehicle. The biggest hurdle was changing gear. That's no problem for you, since like most people in Australia you drive an automatic – and even with my manual gear-box changing gear is no hassle.

But there were no synchromesh gears in those days, so drivers would have to double de-clutch every time they changed gear. And with all the stopping and starting on a bus route they'd be changing gear every few minutes. It was a major problem.

So my father and his colleagues came up with another solution. They connected the petrol engine to an electricity generator. This produced a current that drove the rear wheels – and there's no need to change gear in an electric vehicle.

Today electric-petrol hybrids are hailed as the latest thing, but my father and his colleagues designed the first-ever electric-petrol hybrid over a hundred years ago. It was an engineering triumph.

Ten years after the photograph was taken, the First World War broke out. My father was 32 – the right age to have been sent to fight. But he was not called up because his expertise on motor buses – which were starting to replace horse buses to move the troops in France – was considered so important. *(This is lucky for you and me. The casualties were horrendous. Neither of us would have been here if he had been killed.)*

So now we come back to lodgers, because instead of going to war he took lodgings with my grandmother. And there he fell in love with her daughter Dorothy (she's the two-year old in the photograph, holding a doll and sitting next to her father). They were married in

1917, when she was 20 and he was 34. And that's how I came to be born 13 years later.

There was a song at the time about lodgers:

Our lodger's such a nice young man
Such a nice young man is he
So-o good, so-o kind
To all the fam-il-ee

He's never going to leave us now
Oh dear, oh dear no!
He's such a goody, goody man
Mama told me.

It turned out like that for my grandmother. One of them was so taken by this courageous young widow that he married her. (His surname was Holland – and that's why I've got this odd name 'Holland' as one of my Christian names.) But by this time my grandmother was too old to have any more children – and I should think she was pleased about that.

CHAPTER 12

Time Travelling

My mother's marriage was completely different from *her* mother's because she'd found out how to stop having a child every year – thanks to Marie Stopes. You might think it was the contraceptive pill in the 1970s that made this possible – but the real revolution came years before then when Marie Stopes' book *Married Love* was published in 1918. It sold so fast it had to be reprinted six times in the first fortnight. My mother and father had five happy years together before they decided to start a family. And then, after Thelma was born in 1922 and Rosalind in 1924, they thought that was enough – but they reckoned without me.

It's a chilling thought that these days my mother could have had an abortion. I'm certain they would never have made that choice, but it would have been open to them. I know people who have done just that with an unforeseen child. I know one couple who, hearing the baby was a girl, said: 'Let's terminate it, and try for a boy later.'

I've always felt I was lucky to be alive. Now I feel luckier than ever. But although they planned to have only two children of their own, both my parents had been one of eight children, and had enjoyed being part of a big family. I know you enjoy being one of five and my mother's four sisters were her best friends. When she had to move away from them because of my father's job she missed them. She only had to move just over a hundred miles from her family. Your mother misses her three sisters, but it's several thousand miles from Connecticut to Sydney. And that's another difference between my lifetime and yours. People travel further – and families often end up thousands of miles apart.

When I was growing up in Norfolk, country people did not travel very far from home. They didn't need to. Their families lived close by; there was a school, a church and plenty of shops in their village, and the weekly market in their local town was only a few miles away. Some people would ride to market or hitch up their pony to a cart. Some people cycled – and a lot of them walked. People ride and walk and cycle to keep fit these days – back then they had to ride and walk and cycle to get where they wanted to go. A lot of people who grew up in the Norfolk market towns and villages had never been to Norwich, even though it was only about fifteen miles (24 km) away.

But once it was possible to travel further – by car and eventually by aeroplane – families and communities began to break up. My father had a hand in this. The reason we moved to Norwich in 1930 was that he had been appointed Chief Engineer of the Eastern Counties Bus Company. The company had just been set up to run buses in Norwich – where they soon ousted the trams – and to and from the villages round about. Unlike railway travel, which needed the 'permanent way', buses could travel wherever there was a road. So it was the internal combustion engine in buses, and later on in cars, that enabled people to move away from home and brought an end to a way of life.

It might seem strange to you to blame this on cars, because you've never known a world without them, but it all happened in just one lifetime. I told you that, until my father was 14, a man with a red flag had to walk in front of a car to warn people to get out of the way. By the time he died in 1972 cars were recognisably the same as they are today – and most families could afford one.

Of the thirty families who lived in West Parade when I was a child, only four, apart from us, had a car – the Muriels (who couldn't drive and had a chauffeur), the Bostons, the Suttons and the Boswells. Thelma and I walked up West Parade not long ago when Dorset House was for sale. It was completely cluttered up with parked cars. Each household had one, if not two cars and there was nowhere to put them. No chance of children riding their bikes down there now. *(They were asking £500,000 for Dorset House. I guess my father would have paid something like £500 or £600 in 1930.)*

Our car was a Morris Isis.

It was a tall black car – nearly all cars were black – that had running boards with the spare wheel mounted on the left hand side. A running board is a ledge along the side of the car. You'll have seen some of the new big four-wheel drives now have one, because they are so tall. When my father came home I used to rush out, climb on to the spare wheel and ride on it as he drove round to the garage.

There weren't any locks on the car doors and it didn't have an ignition key. You turned a switch on the dashboard and started it by swinging a handle, which stuck out at the front of the car below the radiator, to turn the engine over. A thermometer on the radiator cap showed the temperature. There was no anti-freeze, and in winter my father would have to drain the radiator every night and fill it up again in the morning. The radiator was a honeycomb pattern, and when my father had been on a long journey there would be moths and wasps stuck in it. There were no traffic indicators. If you were going to turn right, you wound down the window and put your hand out. If you wanted to show you were turning left you circled your arm. Later, in another car we had, little orange arrows stuck out at either side when you flipped a switch. My father belonged to the AA (The Automobile Association). This meant we had a big silver badge on the front of the car and uniformed patrolmen on motor bikes would salute us as we passed.

The seats were dark brown leather and there were deep pockets in the sides of the doors. There were nets fixed to the inside of the roof to keep things in, and a skylight in the centre which opened to let in air. There was no heater and it got very cold in winter, so we always kept travel rugs in the car. There was no boot, and the luggage had to be strapped on a luggage rack which folded down at the back. I think the top speed was 40 mph (65 kph).

We used to travel to London once or twice a year to stay with my aunts. The journey was 120 miles and it took us four hours. There was no radio or CD player in the car. We used to amuse ourselves on the journey by playing I-Spy. There were no motorways, and none of the towns and villages had been by-passed. We drove right through the centre of all of them. Today you can travel at nearly twice the speed (more if you ignore the speed limit), the towns have all been by-passed and motorways built, but there's so much traffic that it will probably take you almost as long as it did back then.

One of the drawbacks of the journey was that all three of us children were travel sick. We used to take one of those enamel potties with us, in case my father couldn't stop the car in time for us to get out.

My father must have been one of the first people to learn to drive, and he taught my mother. There were no driving schools and no driving test. You just got behind the wheel and off you went – like those first bus drivers. A bit different from Australia today, Madison, where you have first to pass a written test and log 100 hours of driving before you can take your test – and then have two different sorts of P plates for three years after you've passed.

I don't think my mother was too bad a driver, but she had a problem reversing. Once she drove into the city centre and, because she hadn't been able to reverse into a parking space, came home, left the car, and went back again by bus. But even so she was more skilled than one of her friends, who had learnt how to change gears up, but not down. She would drive up a hill until the car stalled, then she would put it in first gear and start off again.

We never travelled by train when I was a child, but sometimes we went to meet friends at Thorpe Station. This had a glass roof supported on iron pillars and seemed huge to me. There was a smell of smoke and soot. Because the trains were steam trains and they had big coal fires in the cab to heat the boiler that turned the water into steam. (I seem to remember reading to you about this when you were small, in *Thomas the Tank Engine*.)

The fire made a lot of black smoke, and people who came by train often had sooty smuts on their faces. I loved watching the trains leave. The guard waved a flag and blew his whistle and, as the train moved off, clouds of steam burst out and there was a great whooff! whoff! whoff! as off they went. It used to take two hours to travel the 120 miles to London. Now all the trains are diesel and people don't get covered in soot – but the time is only ten minutes shorter.

Flying was only for the rich when I was a child, but one of my aunts lived in Croydon where there was one of the first 'aerodromes'. The nearest I got to flying was when I was about five, when I was taken to see a plane on the runway. It was very small with a sloping floor, and had seats rather like a bus. No one I knew had ever flown. Aeroplanes could only travel a short distance before refuelling. The way to travel long distances was by sea – on the great new P & O liner Queen Mary, if you were rich enough. I remember my cousins talking about her taking the Blue Riband Trophy for the fastest crossing in 1936. There were no commercial flights across the Atlantic. Planes couldn't carry enough fuel to go that far.

But when I was seven, in 1938, it became possible to fly to and from Australia. The planes were called 'flying boats' because they took off and landed on water. They took off from Sydney Harbour twice a week and arrived in Southampton twelve days later.

During the journey they had to come down to refuel 39 times. They could only fly at a quarter the speed of today's jets – 140 mph (230 kph) as compared with 564 mph (912 kph) and they only flew in daylight. I've got used to those rather strange pre-packaged meals on flights, and dozing uncomfortably in my seat, never quite sure which time zone I'm in. In those days passengers simply went off to a hotel for the night and reported back to the flying boat in the morning. They usually had their meals on the ground, too, but sometimes the steward would serve a three-course meal he had cooked in the galley.

I was talking about the huge changes in cars in my father's lifetime, but they're nothing compared to the changes in air travel in mine. In 1930, the year I was born, Amy Johnson took off from Croydon and flew to Darwin – the first woman ever to fly solo from England to Australia. It took her 21 days. In my lifetime Concorde has crossed the Atlantic in 3½ hours – faster than the speed of sound. Men have landed on the moon and put a space craft on Mars. And – if you're rich enough or to my way of thinking mad enough - you can even be a passenger on space flights, and orbit the earth.

You've already flown thousands of miles, Madison, although you were too small to remember some of the flights. But I'm sure you'll remember visiting your grandparents in Connecticut in September 2001 – and being on the first flight allowed to fly back out of New York to Australia after the World Trade Centre was attacked.

Although flying between England and Australia was much quicker than going by sea in those days – twelve days as compared with six weeks – it was also much more expensive. Now, going by air is the cheap way to travel, and going by sea is the luxury trip. And you might think that, now air travel is affordable, no one would want to go by train unless they had to. But trains are making a comeback. You can now catch a train in the centre of London that gets you to the centre of Paris in a couple of hours. It's faster than flying because you don't have to check in hours beforehand, and you don't have the journey to and from the airport. And in Australia the railway line has been extended so that the luxury train, the Ghan, now runs right through the continent from Adelaide to Darwin.

When I go to Grandparents Day in your little sister's school I meet lots of grandparents who, like me, have travelled thousands of miles. That's not surprising in Australia, which is home to people from all over the world. When I was a child in Norwich most of my school friends' grandparents lived a few streets away.

But things have changed so much that it's quite common for grandparents to live hundreds, if not thousands of miles away. My grandchildren live in Australia. My sister Thelma's live in Texas. Janet Barker, who used to live near us in West Parade, has just been to Poland to celebrate her 80th birthday with her grandchildren there. My friend Margaret's grandchildren live in Spain, and even my friend Patricia – all of whose children live in England – flies from Southampton to visit her grandchildren in the north of England rather than drive for eight hours.

The drawback of this, Madison, seems to me that people don't seem to belong anywhere any more. They have second and third 'homes' and are just 'based' somewhere rather than living there. The next door cottage in my Norfolk village is owned by people who live in New York, and come over once or twice a year. They are really nice people, but the community suffers when there are a lot of absentee owners. So many cottages in the village are now holiday homes that the school and the village shop have both closed because there aren't enough local people to go to them, and the mediaeval church, with its beautiful angel roof, is struggling to find the money for repairs.

But to get back to grandparents and grandchildren, and how far apart they live – the fact that mine lived 100 miles away seems relatively close, compared with today. But by the time I was born my grandparents weren't living anywhere. All four of them were dead.

And that's another difference between then and now, Madison. People live a lot longer.

CHAPTER 13

Mumps & Measles

I can't complain that my parents didn't have long lives. My father was nearly 90 when he died and my mother was 91, but they were far from typical. People didn't live as long as they do now and they were ill more often.

One reason is that there was very little preventive medicine. You've had a lot of injections in your life, although you won't be able to remember most of them because they were given when you were very small, but in my childhood there were virtually none. Vaccination for small pox was compulsory, and I think that's the only one I had. We were all expected to get measles, mumps, chicken pox and whooping cough as children – and we did, and recovered quite quickly.

When your father Oliver was a little boy he was delighted when he was paid a shilling to breathe on a friend's daughter to try to infect her with rubella. *(That's the disease that can cause complications if you get it when you're pregnant, so her parents wanted to make sure she had it when she was a child.)*

In my mother's day children were likely to get typhoid, diphtheria and scarlet fever, all of which could be fatal – *remember Beth in Little Women?* We didn't have injections against those, but they were not nearly as prevalent as they'd been in her day, mainly, I think, because of better hygiene.

There was no injection for polio – which we called 'infantile paralysis' – and from time to time, usually in summer, there was an outbreak. There were two indoor swimming pools in Norwich (I remember once being taken to one on the back of Irene's bicycle) and these were closed if there was an epidemic. Penicillin had not been discovered and neither had streptomycin to cure tuberculosis (TB) – *something that was to affect our lives dramatically in the future.* A boy who lived near us in Mill Hill Road had TB, and he used to spend his days – and nights – in an outdoor summer house his parents had built in the garden, because fresh air was thought to be the best treatment. There were no routine X-rays to detect TB or breast cancer.

There was no National Health (Medicare) and, although there were some free panel doctors, most people paid to see their doctor – so they usually waited until they were ill before they spent the money.

(One reason for free routine check-ups is practical. It costs more to cure people than to keep them healthy. So now the government picks up the bill – via the National Health Service – it's the most cost-effective way of keeping people healthy.)

There were no routine check-ups in my day, and people did not take care of their health in the way they do now. When I stay with you, I see all sorts of people walking and jogging in the early morning – and they swim and cycle. A lot of people in England do too, but not so many. Both your parents go to the gym. Nobody went to the gym in my day. There weren't any – except for professional footballers and boxers – and, of course, in some schools. Places like 'Fitness First' didn't exist.

When I go shopping, I see shelf after shelf of food supplements and vitamins in the supermarkets and in pharmacies. We didn't have them in our day. I once remember having iron tablets, but you couldn't buy these over the counter, they had to be prescribed by the doctor. However, there were a few health foods which my mother was very keen on. *(I've already told you about hiding behind the piano when she came round with these.)*

And there was another reason people were less healthy. The 1930s was the time of the depression.

We were very fortunate that it did not affect us. People were much poorer than they are today; state benefits were minimal and many people didn't get enough to eat. (I told you nobody talked about obesity. People were thin because they were poor.) A lot of children suffered from malnutrition which caused a disease called rickets, so their bones were not strong enough. I saw children wearing iron leg-braces to help their legs take the weight of their bodies.

There have also been huge developments in surgery since my childhood. Many operations which are routine today were unknown. There were no hip or knee replacements, and people who had cataracts simply went blind. And transplants for hearts or lungs or liver were just a dream of the future.

(It is a sobering thought, Madison, that without my two new hips, I should be in a wheelchair, and without routine X-rays to detect cancer, I should not be in a wheelchair, but dead.)

There were no free eye examinations for children and old people, as there are today. There were no contact lenses, and no laser treatments to correct eyesight. Designer frames were unheard of and there were no designer sunglasses. Glasses were boring. Today they can be fun – and I like the ones that go dark in the sun.

I was never taken to the dentist for a six-monthly check-up. People used to wait until they had toothache – by which time it was often too late. A lot of people had gaps in their teeth, or black discoloured teeth. Nearly all older people had false teeth. Dentists just seemed to take teeth out without asking. One day my mother went to the dentist to have a tooth out and found, when she came round from the anaesthetic, that he had taken all her teeth out. She must have been about 37 or 38.

One of the things I notice about you and your friends is that you all have perfect teeth – and I happen to know that your parents have spent a fortune on orthodontics to achieve it. There weren't any orthodontists in my time. The only people who had perfect teeth were the ones whose teeth just grew like that naturally. *(You can tell a horse's age by looking at its teeth, and these days I reckon you can tell a person's age by looking at their teeth, too. If they're over 40, they're a bit of a muddle – but at least the teeth are their own.)*

Another reason we were ill more often is because it's very cold in England, and in winter the temperature is sometimes below freezing for weeks at a time. In Australia you are more concerned with keeping your house cool than keeping it warm. It's the opposite in England. My cottage has double glazing, cavity insulation between the inner and outer brick walls of the house, and thick insulation in the loft. It also has oil-fired central heating plus a wood-burning stove.

There was no insulation in Dorset House and no double glazing. The big sash windows fitted very badly and icy draughts blew in. When we sat round the fire, our faces and front were burning hot and our backs were freezing. We did not have central heating – no one did – and the house was heated by coal fires. But coal fires are not very efficient, most of the heat went up the chimney, and they make an awful lot of work.

(Fires may make an awful lot of work but I still have one, even though with central heating it isn't necessary. It gets dark early in winter and I love sitting beside my wood-burning stove, with my dog Poppy sprawled out on the hearth-rug.)

There was a fireplace in every room at Dorset House, including the bedrooms, but we didn't have a fire in all of them. The fire was always lit in the kitchen and the dining room in winter – and in the nursery in

68

school holidays and weekends. We only lit the drawing room fire when we had visitors.

We hardly ever had a fire in the bedrooms but once, when I was ill, they lit a fire in my bedroom and I still remember how wonderful it was going to sleep with the firelight flickering round the room. But sometimes at night the bedrooms were freezing, literally freezing. As you slept, your breath condensed on the inside of the window pane and in the morning the glass would be frozen over in wonderful patterns.

Have you ever woken up to a fall of fresh snow in the Blue Mountains, Madison? Waking up when it has been snowing in the night is a magical experience. You can tell it has been snowing, because the ceiling of the room is bright from the light reflected off the snow. And when you go to the window to look out, every detail, every little branch and twig and even spider's web has its own delicate filigree of snow. Then there's that wonderful moment when, after porridge for breakfast and wrapped up in scarves and wellies (*which is what we call wellington boots – that's gumboots – in England*) you go out and make the first footprints in the snow.

But being cold means you get coughs and colds more often – you can quite literally catch your death of cold – and every winter we had lots of them. When this happened we used to pour Oil of Eucalyptus on our handkerchiefs and inhale it. *I wonder if it came from Australian eucalyptus trees.* At night we had something called Camphorated Oil rubbed on our backs and fronts (*I think it was supposed to keep out the cold*) and Vick Vapour Rub rubbed on our chests.

Coughs were treated by inhaling Friar's Balsam. My mother put a spoonful of this dark brown stuff into a bowl and poured boiling water over it. Then we sat with our faces over the bowl and towels over our heads and inhaled the steam. We also used to get chilblains, red itchy lumps on your hands and feet, that are caused by the cold.

The temperature in the downstairs rooms of our house in winter was generally about 60F (15C) degrees. It was a lot colder upstairs. That's something else that's different. Your house, like most of the houses in Australia, is open plan, so the temperature is the same in all rooms. Dorset House was divided into separate rooms, and so while the dining room and kitchen (and Irene's bedroom which was above the kitchen) were nice and warm, the rest of the house, even during the day, was sometimes not much above freezing. No wonder we wore lots of clothes – a wool vest, a thin jumper and then a thick one over the top.

(A friend of mine was a vicar's daughter and they lived in a big stone vicarage in the north of England, where it's even colder than in Norfolk. The house was so cold that, when her father left his study to get to the dining room for a meal, he used to put on an overcoat, a hat and a scarf – just to cross the freezing cold hall.)

But even keeping the house at this temperature we still used a ton of coal a month. The coal used to be delivered on a cart drawn by two huge horses. While the coalmen were carrying the sacks of coal round the house and emptying them down the chute into the coal cellar, the horses would wait patiently outside the gate and I would rush out with lumps of sugar for them. They were enormous Shire horses. I had to reach up very high and they would bend their huge heads and take the sugar very gently from my outstretched palm. Their harness had lots of beautifully polished horse brasses hanging from it, and they sometimes had a little brass bell on a bracket between their ears. Their hooves, which were the nearest bits to me, had lots of long fluffy fur round them and were absolutely enormous.

You might think our house was cold, but when I finally went to school – I was five, and it seemed a long wait to me – the rooms were heated by coal fires, too. And it was a lot colder at school than it was at home.

CHAPTER 14

What the Parrot Taught Me

The school year starts in September in England, which is autumn, so it was not too cold to begin with. My first school was called Lonsdale House and it was very near West Parade, so I could walk there with my two sisters in about five minutes. I wore a navy-blue gymslip (a sleeveless tunic) with a woven purple sash round the waist. Under it I wore a white shirt with a striped school tie – schoolgirls always wore a shirt with a tie in those days. In winter a purple jumper went over that. For the walk to school I wore a purple school blazer or, when the weather was colder, a navy-blue mackintosh. I carried a brown leather school satchel.

The school had been started by two sisters some time back in the 1800s when Queen Victoria was still on the throne. The older sister had died, but the younger one was still alive. Her name was Miss Bobbiah *(at least that's how it was pronounced, it might have been spelt Bobbyer, but I'm just going to call her Miss B)*. She had retired and the head of the school was now Miss Callis.

Miss Callis and Miss B. lived in part of Lonsdale House (with two maids to look after them) and the school was in the rest of the house. Although she had retired, Miss B. still appeared from time to time, leaning on a stick and, because she was deaf, carrying an ear trumpet. This was a cone-shaped object about a foot long, and I think it was made of metal. She put the thin end in her ear and you shouted into the fat end and hoped she'd hear.

Miss Callis wore rustling silk dresses with a lot of lace round the throat held in place by a gold brooch. They were both very religious, and we spent a lot of our time singing hymns and rousing choruses. Here's a sample:

> *God has blotted them out!*
> *I'm happy and glad and free!*
> *God has blotted them out*
> *I'll turn to Isaiah and see.*
> *Chapter 44, twenty-two and three*
> *He's blotted them out!*
> *And now I can shout!*
> *For that means me!*

I think it was their ambition to turn us into young ladies. We had to stand up whenever a teacher came into the room and bow slightly when we met them in the corridor – which is the way old-fashioned people used to greet each other. We had needlework lessons on Friday afternoon where we learnt to do embroidery, and also to hem pieces of linen with tiny little stitches. I think this was because fine sewing was considered a ladylike occupation.

This is the schoolroom as it was some time before I went there. By the time I arrived there were individual desks with lift-up lids and a compartment under them. We had to keep a tin of furniture polish in our desks and polish them every week – to turn us into good housewives. Otherwise it was much the same – the same piano and piano-stool, the same clock, the same mirror, the same maps on the wall and the same fireplace. It was really two rooms and twice as big as the part you can see, with another fireplace at the end near the camera.

Lonsdale House was much bigger than Dorset House and, like Dorset House, had tall windows that rattled in the wind. The enormous rooms were heated by coal fires. The teacher would stand in front of the fire, but the rest of us froze – particularly if you sat at the back of the class. We used to wear fingerless gloves to keep our hands warm. These came back into fashion in England at one point, but I don't know if you've ever seen them in Australia. Sometimes it was so cold we could see our breath. That never happens where you live, unless you are up in the mountains.

But it was exciting going to school, and wearing proper school uniform, and being in a big room with lots of other children. Lonsdale was a girls' school but there were two little boys, called Geoffrey Nobbs and Michael Wild in the Kindergarten. They both used to make such a lot of noise that I think Miss Snelling, who taught us, was glad when they left.

You might think it strange that I'd never been in a big group of children until I was five, because when you were quite small you went to Nursery School once or twice a week. In my day there weren't any Nursery Schools or day care centres. Hardly any mothers had a job and children were looked after at home. If a mother did work, she would either have a maid, or sometimes a friend or relation, who had her own child, would look after both children. Not many grannies looked after children. They seemed much older in those days and, as I said, there weren't so many of them left. Today so many mothers work that there are thousands of day care centres – and governments are criticised if they aren't enough of them or if they cost too much.

It was when I visited you during a financial crisis I discovered that childcare is big business. A businessman who owned 1,000 childcare centres in Australia, and the same again in both Britain and America, had to sell shares. The Singapore government (which already owned some shares) bought more – and so did an American bank. Since the tax allowance for childcare is paid direct to the childcare centres, this meant millions of dollars of government subsidies were being used to make money for overseas companies. Then the business went bust. Faced with childcare centres closing, the Australian government felt they had to take responsibility for keeping them open. Looking after little children has changed a lot since Irene and I sat round the kitchen table polishing silver.

But by far the best bit about going to school was learning to read. My sisters had taught me the alphabet and before I was old enough to go to school I used to scrawl letters on a piece of paper and rush up to them asking: 'Is it a word?' So it was a wonderful day when I found out about BAT and CAT and HAT and SAT.

Learning to write was a bit boring because we learnt by using copy books – a sentence is printed and you have to copy it several times – very uninteresting things like:

The quick brown fox jumps over the lazy dog

This style of writing is called copperplate. At first we used pencil, and later a wooden pen with a steel nib which we dipped into an ink well on our desks. We weren't allowed to use fountain pens until we were very much older. Ballpoint pens hadn't been invented. I was a messy child and often went home for our midday meal so covered in ink that I had to have a clean shirt for the afternoon.

We also had to learn a lot of things by heart. First of all we had to learn our multiplication tables and recite them out loud: 'Twice four is eight, three fours are twelve, four fours are sixteen...' and so on, until we knew our twelve times table. (This still happened when your Auntie Lucy was at school in the 1970s. One number she couldn't remember was *'eight eights' so in the end she wrote the number on a piece of paper and ate it. She never forgot it was 64 after that.*)

I know you're good at maths, Madison, but I wonder if you know your multiplication tables, or if you just rely on your calculator? There weren't any calculators in my time. They arrived during the 1970s. They still hadn't been invented when Lucy and Oliver started school in the 1960s.

We also had to learn weights and measures. These are easy now that most countries use kilometres and kilograms, but before decimalisation they were very complicated.

For weights we had to know 16 oz = 1 lb, 14 lb = 1 stone, 28lb = 1 quarter, 56 lb = ½ hundredweight (cwt), 1 cwt = 112 lbs, 20 cwt = 1 ton. For liquids we had to know 4 gills = 1 pint, 2 pints = 1 quart, 4 quarts = 1 gallon.

Measures of length involved links, chains, and rods – all taken from the days when people actually measured with those things. I wonder if you happen to know that an acre is the amount of land a yoke of oxen can plough in a day?

All this information is quite useless since we have changed to using grams and litres and metres, but it seems to me that learning things by heart teaches you to organise things in your mind and develops your mental capacity. I have a theory that it's much the same as walking on a treadmill at the gym. It exercises your heart and develops your muscles – and the fact that you're not actually going anywhere is beside the point. Nowadays learning by heart is called 'parrot fashion' and is out of favour. But children have a huge capacity for it, and the information stays with them for life – it seems a pity not to use it. (*Try me on the Books of the Old Testament – I told you Miss Callis and Miss B. were very religious.*)

We had to learn a poem by heart every week and recite it in class. Nobody found this difficult. I loved it and have gone on doing it ever since. In fact whenever I come across a poem I can't bear to be without, I commit it to memory.

(*I think I told you, Madison, that I've got this wild idea of being marooned on one of those desert islands with just a palm tree in the middle of it, and thinking, if that happened, I must have all the poetry I need, there in my head, to keep me from being miserable.*)

I don't think human memory is like a computer's, which gets full up and has to be emptied. I believe the more you put into it the more it holds.

There were no grounds or playing fields at Lonsdale House, just a gravel yard where we used to rush about at 'break' and where we played netball. Once a week a retired army sergeant, Sergeant Rowe, who had been in the Great War, would come and teach us 'drill'. This meant marching about swinging your arms and doing exercises. He had a large moustache with waxed ends and used to bark out commands in a loud voice. One afternoon a week we would walk in a 'crocodile' (two abreast in a long line) to a playing field to play hockey.

As you can tell, the school was very old fashioned. There was no science teaching and no laboratories. I do not think that many of the teachers had any qualifications, let alone a degree. There was no Sixth Form (Year 11 and 12 in Australia) and we were expected to leave after School Certificate, which is called O levels in England now.

I don't know when School Certificate started, even though I've googled it, but it must have made a big difference to the teaching at the school when it did. After this they had to stick to the syllabus instead of simply trying to turn out young ladies. Because of this I learnt a lot of algebra, geometry (I got as far as Pythagoras with his square on the hypotenuse when I was 11) and geography.

Our geography teaching must have been very different from yours. Big maps of the world hung on the walls of the classrooms and large parts of the world were coloured in pink. This was the British Empire. It was the largest empire in history and people used to say that it was 'the empire on which the sun never set.'

I was a bit hazy about it, but the Empire seemed to consist of some countries that managed their own affairs like Australia, New Zealand and Canada. Then there was India – which had a viceroy because the King was Emperor of India. There was Malaya, Ceylon and Burma (and a few more) in the east. In the west, most of the West Indies were coloured pink, and so were a huge number of countries in Africa. I can remember the names of some of them (*I should know them all if I'd had to learn them by heart)* but it's not much use, since nearly all of them are called something else now they are independent. *(Gaining their independence was thought to be a great step forward. However, when I look round the world today, and see so many of these new nations have corrupt governments, and are in turmoil, with civil war, food shortages and economic chaos, I can only say they don't seem to be better off now they are governing themselves.)*

In geography we also learnt that Mount Everest was the highest mountain in the world and that no one had been able to climb it – and in science that the atom couldn't be split.

The country we knew most about was France. France is a long way from Australia, but it's only about 22 miles (35 km) across the Channel from England. We started to learn French when we were eight. We learnt a lot of French verbs and wrote sentences asking 'Where is the pen of my aunt?' and announcing 'the cat of my father is sitting on the carpet'. (I later found out that at Lonsdale House the teachers' pronunciation wasn't quite the same as it is in France.)

(You once told me you'd studied Japanese at your school. It makes sense to learn the language of countries that are near you. However, it is very convenient for you and me that, because the British Empire stretched over most of the globe, English is the language that is understood nearly everywhere.)

You won't be surprised to hear that my favourite subject was English. As well as learning poetry by heart, we learnt a lot about verbs and prepositions and pronouns – and we had to analyse sentences. We also 'did' Shakespeare – *Romeo and Juliet* and *A Midsummer Night's Dream*. The best bit was when we were taken to see *A Midsummer Night's Dream* at the Maddermarket Theatre (more about this later) and when we had to act bits of it in class. (I also wrote a play *Euphemia Goes to School* and we acted this as well.)

And at home I read all the books I could get my hands on, but I didn't count that as 'doing English'. *(It seems strange to realise now that a lot of the books I read for fun – Sherlock Holmes, Raymond Chandler, Dorothy L. Sayers, P.G. Woodhouse and Alice in Wonderland – are now considered serious literature. I wonder if Frank Richards' Greyfriars School stories and Richmal Crompton's 'William' series, which I read eagerly as each one came out, will ever be called 'classics'?)*

There are three terms in the school year in England – not four as there are in Australia – and at the end of every term we would sing what I found a very puzzling song.

I must explain here that, whereas in Australia 'public school' means one where you don't pay fees, in England 'Public School' means a handful of very expensive boarding schools, among the most famous of which are Eton and Harrow. Eton has a Boating Song, which begins 'Jolly boating weather...', and Harrow has a famous end-of-term song.

For some bizarre reason the little girls of Lonsdale House were made to sing the Harrow song at the end of very term. It goes like this:

> Forty years on when afar and asunder
> Parted are those who are singing today,
> When we look back and forgetfully wonder
> What we were like in out work and our play,
>
> Then it may be there will often come o'er you
> Glimpses of notes, like the catch of a song.
> Visions of boyhood shall float them before you
> Echoes of dreamland shall bear them along.
> Follow up! Follow up! Follow up!
> Till the fields ring again and again
> With the tramp of the twenty-two men.
> Follow up!

Afterwards I would walk back up West Parade wondering who the twenty-two men were, and whether I should meet them. I also wondered if perhaps they were tramps – down-and-outs who begged from door to door.

Fortunately I did not have to spend all my schooldays at Lonsdale House, wondering about the twenty-two men. For, although I enjoyed the school, the trouble was that I learnt more quickly than most of the others, and the school's response was to keep putting me up a form – sometime in the middle of the school year. The result was that, at 12, I ended up in a class of bosomy 14-year-olds giggling about their boy friends and would have taken School Certificate at 14.

But that turned out to be a good thing, because it made me ill. Not very badly. I just got conjunctivitis that took weeks to clear. So my parents decided to send me to another school. This was one of the best things they ever did. But by now I've had enough of school – and I expect you have too – and before I tell you about my next school, I think it would be fun to tell you about what we did in the holidays.

CHAPTER 15

Oil Lamps & Sandcastles

When I was a child, there was no self-catering and no organised camp sites, so most people who could afford to take a holiday would stay in a 'boarding house' in a seaside town. This meant the whole family would live as lodgers in someone's house. You were expected to go out after breakfast and not come back until it was time for an evening meal – for which you paid extra. If you were rich enough you might stay in a seaside hotel. We never did, but one of my father's business associates used to stay in the Grand Hotel in Sheringham, and every summer we used to be invited to lunch. It was terrifying. There was a huge expanse of starched white tablecloth waiting to have things spilt on it, an enormous number of knives and forks, waiters who put strange food on your plate and, if you were a slow eater, took it away before you had finished it. Most puzzling of all were little bowls of water, which were meant for washing your fingers in. Nearly all the Grand Hotels have been pulled down now and flats built in their place.

I was only taken to seaside boarding houses when I was very small, because one day, when we were driving along the coast at a place called Eccles, my sister Thelma saw a notice 'Seaside Bungalows for Sale' and persuaded my parents to drive down a little lane to have a look at them. A farmer had sold some fields beside the sea to a Norwich builder, and he had built a whole estate of bungalows there. There were no planning regulations then. You could build what you liked, where you liked. The prices started at £100 (a tenth of my father's annual income). As soon as they saw them, my parents made up their minds. They bought one of the bungalows shortly afterwards, and called it Tresillian after the road where they lived so happily when they were first married. I think it must have been in 1935 – if so, I would have been four years old that summer.

A flight of wooden steps led out of our back garden up over the sand dunes directly onto the beach. At night you could hear the waves breaking on the shore. Best of all, since Eccles is about 20 miles (32 km) from Norwich, my father could drive to work. This meant we could spend the whole of the summer holidays at the beach *(school summer holidays in England last six weeks)* and could spend the Easter holidays there too, if it was warm enough.

The bungalow was built of wood and had four rooms – a big sitting room with doors onto a veranda, two bedrooms and a kitchen. It also had a flat roof where you could sunbathe.

Thelma and Irene (Irene came with us, of course) slept in one bedroom, Rosalind and I slept in another, and my parents slept on a settee in the sitting room. The walls were lined with asbestos sheeting – nowadays illegal because it is a health hazard.

There was no electricity, no water supply and no flush lavatory at the bungalow. This did not seem strange to us. As I've told you, in those days a great many cottages in the country, where people lived permanently, did not have these things. Irene's parents were quite happy with oil lamps, a well for water, an earth closet lavatory and a coal-fired stove.

There was no fireplace for a cooking stove at Eccles, and so we had a paraffin stove. It had two burners and you could put an oven on top. We had oil lamps and candles for light. In summer in England it doesn't get dark until 10 o'clock, so we didn't often need them. We got electricity after a year or two and had electric lights and an electric cooker, which I did not think was so much fun. The electricity company didn't send us a bill. We had a meter and paid for the electricity by putting shillings into it. When the money ran out the power went off.

Instead of an earth closet we had an Elsan chemical toilet in a shed beside the house. I don't know if you've come across these. There is an outer container with a toilet seat on it and a removable inner container with a strong chemical in it. You can just see the  corner of it at the left of the photo and there's our car on the right.

Our toilet – and all the others on the estate – was emptied once a week by a man called Mr Cutting (whose daughter later came to work for us). Goodness knows how he disposed of the contents. Tipped it into the sea, is my guess. Going to the loo wasn't pleasant – so of course we used those chamber pots and then emptied them into the garden. *(Sorry about this disgusting detail. As you see, history and plumbing are often connected.)*

We didn't have our own well, as Irene's parents did, but the builder had sunk a well to serve all the bungalows. We didn't have to let down a bucket to get the water, it came gushing out when you pumped the handle of a big iron pump. One of the jobs my sisters and I had to do each day was fetch water. Thelma and Rosalind had big enamel jugs and I had a little one. We also had a five-gallon container. This was quite heavy, so either my sisters would carry it between them, or we would leave it at the pump for my father to bring in the car when he came home from work.

At the beginning of the holidays my father would strap our bicycles onto the back of the car and take them to Eccles. They were useful because we had to fetch the milk as well as the water. This didn't come in bottles, but more or less straight from the cow. We cycled up the lane – we called it Foggy Lane because of the dust the car raised when we drove along it – to a farm on the top road. Mrs Pestle the farmer's wife would take us into the dairy – a cool room with a wonderful smell and a brick floor – and scoop the milk out of a bowl into our billycan. Then we would cycle back home with the can on our handlebars.

Of course a great deal of our time was spent on the beach. Norfolk is not nearly as warm as Australia, but we swam nearly every day. Our swim suits were made of wool, which takes ages to dry. Wool also gets very heavy when it is wet and sags. *(It's a bit different from your bikini, which is the size of a postage stamp and dries in seconds as you sun yourself on Bondi Beach.)*

Talking of sunning yourself reminds me that you always put on lots of Factor 30 Sunscreen before you go out in the sun. There wasn't any sunscreen in my day, and we didn't know how harmful the sun could be. On the first days of the holidays our skin would get red and painful. Then the skin would flake off and peel. And after that we would begin to develop a tan. Even in the 1980s I used to sunbathe without sunscreen. *(I sometimes say that's why my face is so wrinkly now – but I'm afraid it's just old age.)*

The water was very cold compared with your beaches, and after we'd swum we would have to wrap up warmly afterwards *(just imagine having to do that in Australia)* and we built sandcastles and flew kites. I never seemed to manage to get my kite off the ground – in the same way that my yo-yo always seemed to go to the bottom of the string and stay there.

We didn't surf, of course, because the waves in the North Sea aren't the right sort. But there are lots of shrimps there, which are like tiny prawns. We all had shrimping nets and used to walk backwards and forwards in the sea, pushing them in front of us.

My father had a huge shrimping net, and he and my big cousins would wade waist-deep in the sea with their nets and catch masses of them. We would take the live shrimps home, boil them in sea water and have them for tea.

This is the first time you've met my cousins. I had eleven of them altogether, and they all lived in London. We sometimes used to go and visit them in London. But after we bought the bungalow at Eccles we saw a lot more of them, because my mother's two younger sisters, Auntie Estelle and Auntie Jo, used to rent a bungalow near us for two weeks every summer. (If you look at the Victorian photograph, you'll see Auntie Estelle is the little girl on her mother's knee in the photograph. Auntie Jo hadn't been born.)

Neither of my aunts had a car, and they couldn't drive in any case, so my father used to go to London to collect them and bring them back to Eccles. Somehow an extra two adults and six children all crammed into our Morris Isis, with their luggage in a trunk on the back. There were no seat belts in those days and no restrictions on how many people you could cram in.

My uncles couldn't get away to join their families. Auntie Estelle's husband, Uncle Morgan, had a newsagents and tobacconists shop and he couldn't shut it, even for a week. He sold cigarettes, which were very cheap in those days, and he used to smoke a lot. He died of lung cancer. People didn't realise then how bad smoking is for you.

The two aunts had six children between them. Five of them – a girl and four boys – were about the same age as my sisters. There was also a little girl my own age. I was meant to play with her but, sad to say, we took a dislike to each other on sight.

The boys flung themselves into the holidays. They took proper garden spades down to the beach and built enormous sand castles. We swam, and played beach cricket, and 'polo' on bicycles with croquet mallets, and sometimes we cycled off to proper tennis courts nearby. When it was wet we played endless card games and guessing games.

I was always quite pleased when they went back home, and I felt a bit mean when, years later, the oldest boy told me 'those were my golden years'.

My aunts wore black woollen bathing costumes like my mother's when they went swimming and I think, looking back, that they felt a bit shy wearing them. I expect they had bought them especially for the holidays. When they were children, bathing costumes had long sleeves and frilly skirts. If their mother (the one in the photograph) had gone to the beach she would have worn a long skirt, shoes and stockings, hat and gloves – but I shouldn't think she ever did that, or possessed a bathing costume, in her entire life.

I expect you know that in Australia it was illegal to swim during the daytime until 1903 – young men used to swim naked, and the law was passed to stop them. But even at Eccles in the 1930s my father wore a bathing costume with a top, rather like my mother's, not swimming trunks.

We had very simple meals when we lived at the beach – if we'd been in Australia we would have had barbecues, but nobody had them in England then. Most of our food came from Mr Clements' shop.

Mr Clements kept the village shop in Lessingham, the nearest village to Eccles. It sold everything you can think of. There were sacks of flour and sugar (often with a black cat sitting on them), shelves of cans and bottles, piles of saucepans and garden tools, vests and knickers. Hams and overcoats hung from the ceiling – there was even a Post Office in one corner. When the bungalows were built at Eccles, Mr Clements started a shop there, too.

The things my sisters and I bought mostly were sweets – acid drops, aniseed balls, liquorice sticks, toffees, caramels, chocolate drops, sticks of rock, jelly babies, bulls' eyes, humbugs, sherbet, chewing gum, nougat. They mostly came in tall glass jars. You could buy a pennyworth or a ha'pennyworth, and Mr Clements would measure them out into a little white bag. He also sold kites, beach-balls, shrimping nets and buckets and spades. The buckets and spades were made of tin – not plastic. I was only allowed a wooden spade, not a metal one, in case I cut my toes off. My mother and my aunts bought tins of soup and baked beans and corned beef and ham – and other things to make a quick meal.

Mr Clements' shop didn't have a fridge or a freezer and he didn't sell fish and meat – and there were no frozen foods. But the local butcher came round with a van, and so did the fishmonger. And there was a curly-headed boy aged about 17 who brought great trays of raspberries and strawberries, freshly picked from the local farms, in a battered Austin Seven van. We called him 'the raspberry boy' and my oldest girl cousin thought he was very dashing. We used to tease her by singing one of the popular songs, substituting 'raspberry boy' for 'butcher's boy':

Tell me why he winks his eye
Whenever he goes by my window
It's the butcher's boy
And he's a parcel in his hand.

Oh, Ma, Ma, get that man for me!
Oh Ma, Ma, how happy I shall be!
Oh Ma, Ma, oh dearie, dearie me!
The butcher's boy, the butcher's boy,
The butcher's boy for me!

Mr Clements' shop had his name E. CLEMENTS written in white paint on the roof, and my aunts used to call the shop Ecclements. Eccles must have been a great adventure for them. They giggled a lot, and used to ride my mother's bicycle – and sometimes fell off. Both of them had lived all their lives in London and they were not used to the country. Once, when we were walking up Foggy Lane, a farm worker, leading a large Shire horse, came along on his way back to the farm. Auntie Jo screamed, scrambled up the bank and hid behind a hedge until they were past. Very embarrassing!

CHAPTER 16

Hedgerows & Harvest

We weren't frightened of horses even though we lived in the city because, unlike our aunts, we saw a lot of them. It wasn't just George's horse when he brought the groceries, and the huge Shire horses that brought the coal. We used to go for lessons at a riding school run by Stella Nightingale. Stella was broad and sturdy with straight dark hair, which was short and cut in a fringe – not permed like my mother's and her friends'. She was very good at riding and always wore jodhpurs, jodhpur-boots and a short-sleeved shirt – and she had strong hands and freckled arms. When I grew up I didn't want to be a mannequin in Garlands any more, as I did when I was very small. I wanted to be like Stella Nightingale and have a riding stable.

During the summer Stella Nightingale moved her horses to Bacton, which was just along the coast from Eccles, and kept them in the stables of The Ship Inn.

(Bacton used to be a little fishing village, but when gas was discovered in the North Sea, it became the place where it was piped ashore. Now there is a huge terminal there and Bacton is quite unrecognisable.)

We used to go for long rides, one behind the other, with Stella in front. Stella always rode a chestnut horse called 'Unexpected' which often used to try to buck her off – but it never managed it. Towards the end of the summer, when the harvest was over, we would canter on the stubble fields, and have 'bending races' in and out of the stooks of wheat. Sometimes we would ride on the beach *(you're not allowed to do this in summer any more)* where we would ride the horses into the sea. Once 'Unexpected' decided to go for a swim.

Sometimes we would ride on bridle paths – one of which ran through the ruins of what seemed to be a great church. Later I found that this was all that was left of the Abbey of Bromholme – famous throughout Europe in the Middle Ages because it had a relic of the True Cross.

And sometimes we would take sandwiches and spend the whole day at the stables, which I thought was heaven, and we would clean tack and muck out.

When we rode out, Stella used to wear a hacking jacket and a pork pie hat (like George who delivered the groceries) and we were bareheaded or wore a sunhat. Nobody wore a hard hat to go riding in those days, except people who went hunting. *(When you used to ride in the Blue Mountains, I'm sure they would not let you get on a horse unless you had a hard hat. Even so, I'm told that the insurance has become so costly that a lot of stables have had to close because they can no longer afford it.)*

The lanes we rode through were ablaze with wild flowers, and so were the farm tracks that stretched for miles around our bungalow. The hedges were thick with blossom – hawthorn in early summer, wild roses later – and there were birds' nests with tiny eggs in them in the spring. And there were beautiful butterflies. I've seen wonderful butterflies in Australia – big black ones with white spots, almost as big as a bird. Our English ones were smaller, but their colours were bright as jewels – Red Admirals, Purple Emperors, Swallowtails, Tortoiseshells, Brimstones, and a lot more whose names I can't remember. It was a time when children could roam out of doors all day long with no one to keep an eye on them.

We used to bicycle along the lanes for hours, and pick great bunches of wild flowers to take home. My sister Thelma got really interested in them and wanted to know their names – so for one of her birthdays I bought her a book, *Wild Flowers of the Wayside and Woodland*, which identified them. After that we would bring them home, put them between pieces of blotting paper, and put them under the carpet to press them. When they were dried we stuck them in a book and wrote their names beside them. We used a roll of sticky paper – cellulose tape had not been invented. The wild flowers were glorious in those days, and the scent of them filled the summer air. I know the names won't mean anything to you, Madison, but just listen to some of them – lady's bedstraw, saxifrage, speedwell, pimpernel, eyebright, valerian, woodruff, lady's mantle, ragged robin, jack-by-the-hedge, corn cockle, creeping jenny, lords-and-ladies.

And there were some not-so-romantic names – stinking hawk's beard, scurvy grass, toad flax and viper's bugloss. In springtime there were great drifts of bluebells and cowslips and primroses.

And in summer (much to the farmers' disgust) there were great patches of scarlet poppies among the wheat. People still call Norfolk 'Poppyland' today.

I know people romanticise the past, Madison, but I can prove I'm not making this up, because I've still got a copy of the wild-flower book and in it there are hundreds, literally hundreds, of wild flowers. There are forty-one varieties of wild orchids alone. And during the next few years we managed to find all the flowers in the book – all except one, snake's head fritillary.

The reason I'm going on at such length about this is that nowadays virtually all of them have disappeared. The farmers wanted to get rid of the poppies in the wheat field – together with all the rest of the 'weeds' – and chemical weed-killers were invented to do it. And the spray drifted from the fields and killed the wild flowers. When I went back to Foggy Lane thirty years later, the riot of colour had gone and all I could find was hogweed, nettles and cow parsley. Wild flowers have become so scarce in England that it is now illegal to pick them.

(I don't know many of your Australian wild flowers, but I find it amusing that the wonderful blue Morning Glory, which is treasured in England, is such a menace in the Australian bush that people are forbidden to grow it. It's even stranger that privet – which in England is so much a byword for suburban respectability that Harry Potter's dreadful Dursley relations live in Privet Drive – goes wild when it gets to Australia and goes on the rampage, so it has to be exterminated.)

Although we knew the country a lot better than my London aunts, we got to know it even better once we began to spend our summers at Eccles. When we cycled up Foggy Lane to get our milk, we would sometimes meet the cows coming back to the field after being milked by hand. Now they are milked by machine in milking parlours in the field and it's rare to meet a herd of cows on the road as we often did in the old days.

We understood that the horses that frightened our aunts were quite literally the horse-power on the farms in those days before tractors. They pulled the farm carts – they are still called 'tumbrils' in Norfolk, just like the carts that took the French aristocrats to the guillotine in the French Revolution. And horses pulled all the rest of the farm machinery – the harrows and the seed drills and the ploughs.

Before the days of tractors, ploughing was hard work – and it took great skill to get the furrows straight. The ploughman would walk backwards and forwards across the field all day, stepping over the furrow made by the plough, and turning the horses on the 'headland' at each end of the field.

No wonder Thomas Gray wrote:

'The ploughman homeward plods his weary way.'

This postcard shows one of the ploughmen from Mr Pestle's farm with a three-horse plough at Eccles with some of the older bungalows in the back-ground.

The fields were ploughed in spring-time, ready for the seed to be sown, when we were at Eccles for Easter.

We were always at Eccles for harvest time in August, and we used to go and watch as the horses pulled the reaper and binder round the field. This machine was a recent invention and was a great advance on cutting the wheat with a sickle and binding it by hand. The older men getting in the harvest would have cut wheat by hand in their time. They wore thick woollen trousers, kept up by braces and tied with string at the knees, a striped shirt with no collar, and a neckerchief round their throats. It was very dusty work, and their wives would bring bottles of cold tea out to them in the harvest field.

As the reaper and binder went round the field, the rabbits would run into the centre. When the last of the field was cut they would run out. The boys would hit them on the head with sticks – and everyone would have rabbit pie for supper. After the harvest the chickens and geese would be turned onto the fields, with the children to keep an eye on them, to have a feed on the grain that had fallen.

There was work for everyone at harvest time, and we used to help on Mr Pestle's farm and stack the wheat sheaves, eight at a time, into stooks – they are called 'shoaves' and 'shocks' in Norfolk. These stood in the field until the ears (the seeds) had dried. Then a cart, pulled by a great Shire horse with a little boy perched on top, would go round the field, and the men would toss the sheaves into the cart and take them for threshing, to separate the wheat from the straw. Not many years earlier, they did this by throwing it on the floor of a barn and beating it with flails (another very hot and dusty job). But now there was a machine that did the threshing. The wheat was collected in sacks, and the men carted the straw away and threw it up with a pitchfork to make big stacks.

Now huge combine harvesters roar across the fields, cutting and threshing in one operation. The straw is baled up into squares or enormous rolls. The hedges, where the birds used to nest, have been pulled out to make the fields big enough for the machinery to work. Enormous tractors pull the ploughs instead of horses. Farm machinery now costs so much that a lot of farmers are in debt to pay for it – and the European Union has introduced such a lot of regulations that the paperwork is so complicated it takes hours to cope with it. People talk about farming as 'the industry' now, and you can see why.

After the harvest there was always a Harvest Thanksgiving in the little flint church at the top of Foggy Lane. The church would be decorated with sheaves of wheat, and there would be enormous vegetable marrows and great piles of fruit round the font. Afterwards there would be a harvest supper for the farm workers. We weren't invited to that, but we joined them in church and sang:

> *We plough the fields and scatter the good seed on the land*
> *But it is fed and watered by God's Almighty hand*
> *He sends the snow in winter, the warmth to swell the grain*
> *The breezes and the sunshine, and soft, refreshing rain*
> *All good gifts around us are sent from heaven above*
> *So thank the Lord, O thank the Lord, for all his love.*

Farming had been carried on like this for centuries and we didn't know this way of life was going to end. None of us did – not even the poets, who usually get things right. Thomas Hardy wrote:

> *Only a man harrowing clods*
> *In a slow silent walk*
> *And an old horse that stumbles and nods*
> *Half asleep as they stalk*
>
> *Only thin smoke without flame*
> *From the heaps of couch grass*
> *This will go onward the same*
> *Though dynasties pass*

But it's gone, and will never come back. I was so lucky to be born in time to catch a glimpse of it before it disappeared for ever.

CHAPTER 17

Goodbye to All That

We didn't know it, but after our holiday at Eccles in 1939, a lot of other things were going to disappear. I was eight years old, and world events meant nothing to me, but I had read the word CRISIS on the newspaper placards, and I knew my parents were worried when we packed up the bungalow to come back to West Parade.

The first Sunday after we got back, my parents didn't come to church with us. They stayed behind to listen to the wireless (which is what we called the radio). When we came back they told us that war had been declared. I had no idea what this would mean, but I heard them saying to each other: 'Not like the last lot.'

You've studied the 1914-18 war, and seen film of it, and read Wilfred Owen's poetry. I've even got some of it tucked away in my memory for when I'm on that desert island:

> *What passing bells for these who die as cattle?*
> *Only the monstrous anger of the guns*
> *Only the stuttering rifle's rapid rattle*
> *Can patter out their hasty orisons.*
> *No mockery now for them; no flowers no bells*
> *Nor any voice of mourning save the choirs*
> *The shrill demented choirs of wailing shells*
> *And bugles calling for them from sad shires.*
> *What candles may be held to speed them all?*
> *Not in the hands of boys, but in their eyes*
> *Shall gleam the holy glimmers of goodbyes*
> *The pallor of girls' brows shall be their pall*
> *Their flowers the tenderness of patient minds*
> *And each slow dusk a drawing down of blinds.*

But very few people had read Owen until years afterwards, when Benjamin Britten used it for his *War Requiem* in 1962, and the newsreel film was tucked away in the archives.

I think people wanted to forget it had ever happened. My parents never talked about it. Years later I found out that my mother's brother Seymour – the good-looking boy standing at the back of the photograph – was killed at the Somme in July 1916. She never mentioned it.

What the war meant to me was that we could not go to Eccles any more. All the area near the coast, for several miles inland, was declared a 'restricted area' which no one could visit without a permit. My parents were allowed to bring the furniture home from the bungalow. The army put up scaffolding covered with razor wire on the sand dunes, and laid mines on the beach where we used to play. All the bungalows were requisitioned for soldiers to live in.

Back home we all had to be fitted with gas masks. They smelt of rubber and made a funny noise as you breathed out. They came in a cardboard box with a string handle, and we bought waterproof cases with a shoulder strap to put them in. I carried my gas mask everywhere I went for the next five years. We were also issued with identity cards and we each had a metal identity bracelet with our name and identity number (mine was TPOK 135/5) engraved on it, so that if we were killed people would know who we were (or had been).

Everyone thought that London would be bombed at once, and so Auntie Estelle and Auntie Jo and the cousins came to stay with us in Norwich. But after a few weeks with no raids they went back to London. I think my aunts didn't want to leave their husbands on their own, and decided if they were going to be in danger, they would face it together.

They did. There were very heavy raids in Croydon and Bromley where they lived later on. Their older sister Auntie Pat (standing on the left in the old photograph) suffered the worst. Her father-in-law was the Master of the West India Dock and they lived in Poplar, where the docks were heavily bombed night after night.

Because of the risk of air raids we had the 'blackout', which meant we were not allowed to have lights shining after dark. *(You've flown over cities at night, Madison, so you know how clearly they show up from the air.)* All the street lights were switched off, car headlights were fitted with masks that only let out a little light – even torches were masked. My mother made thick curtains for the rooms we often used and my father made wooden frames to fit the rest of the windows and tacked thick paper onto them.

He also had a big air raid shelter, made of reinforced concrete, built in our garden. Some of our friends had Anderson shelters, which were made of corrugated iron sheets and set in a hole in the ground, and some had a Morrison shelter, which was like a big table made of steel. They put this in their living room and sat inside it during a raid, so that they would be protected even if the house collapsed around them. The city council built public air raid shelters in a lot of the streets. One day my mother met Daisy Osborne looking at the shelter in Mill Hill Road, at the back of West Parade, to see if she could take her mother there.

At once my mother said they must come and share ours, so when the air raid siren sounded, Mrs Osborne with her daughters Daisy and Mabel, wrapped in blankets, would come and join us in the shelter. *(We had scarcely spoken to them in the eight years that we had been neighbours, which you might think strange. But people used to 'keep themselves to themselves' in those days. I think it was because families were much closer and other people were regarded as outsiders. Australians seem much more open to other people. Do you think it is because so many of them have left their families behind them when they come to live in Australia?)*

Once we got to know the Osbornes we found they were great fun. I can't remember what we talked about (except one hilarious conversation about old-fashioned knickers) but I remember us falling about with laughter – which seems odd when there were ack-ack (anti-aircraft) guns going off and German bombers overhead. Their mysterious son – the one who didn't speak to anyone – never joined them. They never mentioned him and we didn't even know his name. I suppose he just stayed in the house and hoped for the best.

After we became friends, Daisy used to go to the cinema with my sister Rosalind – something I feel sure she had never done before – and I used to go and help Daisy cut her garden hedge (yes it was privet) and stay to tea afterwards.

The school term started a few days after war was declared. My sister Thelma was 17 and decided not to go back to school, but to take a secretarial course and learn shorthand and typing. She learnt to type on a manual typewriter. You had to hit each key with the same pressure, or the letters looked uneven. A bell rang to warn you when you were getting near the end of the line, and then you had to push a lever to get back to the left hand side of the page and move up to the next line. It was possible to tell which make of typewriter was used, and even which individual machine. *(Just see how many times this turns up in old detective stories – from Sherlock Holmes right through to Rumpole of the Bailey.)* If you wanted more than one copy you had to use carbon paper between the sheets of paper, and if you made a mistake you had to rub it out with a rubber. Can you imagine how accurate you had to be? Now everyone can turn out accurate typescript on a computer – even your little sister Zoe aged 7. In any case hardly anyone writes letters any more – they send emails.

My sister Rosalind and I went back to school at Lonsdale House. We found that strips of sticky paper had been criss-crossed over the windows so that, if they were shattered by bomb-blast, the pieces would stick together and not be so likely to injure people. The roof of the cloakrooms had been shored up with beams of timber to strengthen them to make an air raid shelter, and there were buckets of sand and stirrup pumps in the corridors to use to put out fires.

There was a new girl in my form called Olga Lenck who had come from Germany. Until then I had never met anyone from a country outside England. She was very pale and hardly spoke any English. She and her brother were living with a family in Norwich, but she did not know where her parents were. We were all anxious to help her and be her friend. There were German girls in other forms, too. I remember part of a song from that time about a Dutch boy and girl:

My sister and I recall the day
We said goodbye and then sailed away
And we think of our friends who had to stay
But we don't talk about that

We're trying to forget the fear
That came from a troubled sky
We're almost happy over here
But sometimes we wake at night and cry.

(One of the people who had to stay behind in Holland was Anne Frank. When she began her diary – on her thirteenth birthday in 1942 – she was about a year older than me, and had less than three years to live. Her Diary is famous now and I know you've read it, but of course it wasn't published until years later. Reading it now makes me realise, even more vividly, what a narrow escape we had.)

At the beginning of the war my father cut a map of Europe out of one of the newspapers and mounted it on hardboard. With the map there were little flags of all the countries mounted on pins, and we stuck these on the map to show how the war was going. By the summer of 1940 there were only German flags on mainland Europe. The whole of Europe had been overrun and our defeated army had been rescued by the armada of little ships that sailed to Dunkirk. In Norfolk this meant there were only about 45 miles (72 km) between us and the conquering German army.

The weather was glorious that summer of 1940. Rosalind and I often went riding – Thelma couldn't come because she was at work. Our parents said that income tax was going to go up to 10 shillings in the pound (50%), which was a huge increase, to pay for the war – and we had better go while they could still afford it. Stella Nightingale had moved her stables inland to Swanton Abbot, and we used to catch a bus from Norwich into the country, where Stella would meet us with a pony and trap. (A trap is a little open horse-drawn carriage. This one had faded velvet cushions and was drawn by a shaggy little Shetland pony.) There were several airfields near Swanton Abbot and, as we rode, the skies seemed to be filled with aircraft. Though I didn't realise it, the Battle of Britain was being fought overhead.

Five of my cousins turned 18 in 1940. If you were a boy, turning eighteen didn't mean a special party – twenty-one was the age of majority – it meant getting your call-up papers, telling you to join the army. I had eleven cousins altogether – eight of them boys. All of them were called up – except one, who failed the medical exam. My mother was the only one of the five sisters who didn't have a son. Looking back, I should think she was pleased about this – perhaps for the first time.

Girls weren't called up. My sister Thelma wanted to join the WAAF (Women's Auxiliary Air Force) but girls under 21 had to have their parents' permission and my parents wouldn't let her. She joined the ARP. (This stood for Air Raid Precautions and was part-time.) When the siren went she put on her uniform and ran down West Parade to a house there that had been taken over as ARP headquarters. Two 17-year-old schoolboys also reported there. Their job was to cycle through the city to take messages if bombs had put the telephones out of action. They told some hair-raising stories of cycling through streets with burning buildings all around them. (*I rather think your brother Carson might have enjoyed this if he'd had the opportunity.*) When these boys turned 18 they were called up. One of them went into the army, but the other was sent down the coal mines. (I think the names for this were chosen out of a hat.) These lads were called 'Bevin boys' after the Minister of Labour, Ernest Bevin. When he came home he told us they still had pit ponies down the mines.

My mother joined the Red Cross and read lots of books on First Aid. She really enjoyed having a worthwhile job to do and made lots of new friends. She and her friends would practice on me when I came home from school. I had my arms in slings, my legs in splints, my feet, hands, head and neck bandaged until I looked like an Egyptian mummy. Fortunately I don't think they ever had to do this with real casualties. My mother used to go to the

hospital to help with blood donors, and helped run a canteen at the railway station for servicemen who were passing through. At first these were British servicemen, but after the Germans had overrun Europe, there were all sorts of nationalities – Poles, and French, and Czech and Dutch and Belgians. The streets of Norwich were soon full of people in uniform.

Our great excitement came when a Canadian Army officer, who was a nephew of our next door neighbours Dr and Miss Muriel, came to stay with them when he was on leave. *(We got to know the Muriels better during the war, too.)* They were at a loss as to how to entertain a young man, and so they sent him next door to us. He used to tell us stories about his home in the Canadian Rockies, which seemed wonderfully exotic to us. *(Now you ring your cousins in America without a thought and feel quite at home there when you go and stay with them.)*

We only knew Canada and America from the cinema, and we had never met anyone who lived in either country. But that changed after December 1941 when the Americans came into the war after the attack on Pearl Harbour. Norfolk is very flat, so it is a good place to build airfields, and soon Norwich was full of American airmen who were stationed at the many airfields round about.

If you knew one of them, you could get nylon stockings and chewing gum, but my parents got worried when my sister went out with them. Perhaps they thought that, whatever the Americans had in mind in exchange for nylons, it wasn't marriage.

But a lot of them did marry local girls. One of them was Irene's younger sister Agnes – the older of the two bridesmaids in Irene's wedding photograph.

After the war she was one of the two thousand GI brides who sailed away on the Queen Mary to a new life in America. It was a huge step for someone who had never travelled more than a few miles from home and her family must have been very anxious she might not be happy so far away from them in South Carolina. But all was well. In the years that followed, Agnes and her husband often came back to England and I met them several times. The last time I saw them, they were celebrating their 60th wedding anniversary. So, yes, I'm able to tell you that their dream came true, and they really did live happily ever after.

CHAPTER 18

Bombs in West Parade

'Living happily ever after' was something we kept looking forward to once the war was over. You may have heard the song Vera Lynn used to sing:

There'll be bluebirds over
The white cliffs of Dover
Tomorrow, when the world is free

But even though we were continually thinking about how different life would be in the post-war world, our immediate concern was staying alive in the present.

The coast of occupied France was only about 45 miles (72 km) away from Norwich, and we were on the route for German bombers flying over to bomb the industrial towns in the Midlands. So most nights there would be two Air Raid Warnings – once when they came over and once when they came back. If they had any bombs left, they would drop them on Norwich. The Air Raid Warning was a siren with a wailing sound. There was also a Crash Warning – a series of short hoots, which meant that danger was imminent.

When the siren went we would put on the warm clothes we used to keep ready at the end of our beds and dash to the shelter, where we'd stay until we heard the All Clear, which was a single note. Then we'd come out into the cool night air – sometimes it smelt of burning – and go back to bed. If the All Clear did not go until after 2 am we were allowed to get to school at 9.30 instead of 9 o'clock.

During most of the raids there was the sound of anti-aircraft fire and quite a few bombs were dropped, but Norwich was never a serious target. Not, that is, until April 1942.

Then Hitler got the bright idea that, if they were to destroy some of England's most beautiful buildings, the morale of the people would be shattered. (These were called the Baedeker raids after the name of the famous German guide book.)

'Morale' was a new word to me, but I soon found out what it meant. You might think that, if people are trying to invade your country and to kill you, you would be frightened and miserable and discouraged. Not a bit of it. It makes you absolutely determined that nothing will get you down. However this was something the Germans didn't seem to understand and they set out to destroy Norwich Cathedral.

(You won't remember Norwich Cathedral from when you lived in Norwich, Madison. It's a glorious building in the centre of Norwich, which was founded nearly a thousand years ago. We lived in the Cathedral Close when your father Oliver and Auntie Lucy were growing up, and your parents were married in the Cathedral.)

On 27th April 1942 the German Luftwaffe came in force to bomb Norwich. That night, my father was fire-watching at his office at the other side of the city. Fire-watching didn't mean sitting round a cosy fire. When buildings were left empty at night people took it in turns to stay up and keep a lookout so that, if incendiary bombs fell, they could either put them out with sand and a stirrup pump, or call the Fire Brigade before the fire got a hold.

There were no Air Raid Warning that night – just the Crash Warning which meant that danger was imminent. We woke to such a terrific sound of bombs exploding and gunfire that we daren't run across the garden to the shelter. Thelma had no time to get to the ARP post. My mother, Thelma, Rosalind and I ran to the china pantry, which was the strongest part of the house. The china pantry was under the Big Spare Bathroom Cupboard where we stored all our junk. I had visions of the beds from Eccles, the doll's house and my old pram tumbling down on top of us if the house was hit.

For two or three hours we sat there, huddled on the floor with our arms around each other, while the house rocked and there was a deafening series of explosions. At last it was quiet. The All Clear sounded and we crept out.

The house was still standing and, amazingly, no windows were broken – because perhaps the sashes fitted so loosely they had room to vibrate. Everywhere was filthy. Soot had been blown down the chimney, and the whole house was thick with dirt and dust. No water came out of the taps, the lights didn't work, and neither did the gas.

My father got home to find us all safe. He was shaking and out of breath. As he drove home through the city he had passed bomb craters and devastation everywhere. The big wood yard near the railway station had been set on fire and flames were leaping into the sky. A lot of the roads he usually took were blocked. When he got to West Parade it was impassable. He left the car and ran, not knowing what he would find.

Three bombs had been dropped in West Parade. Two houses had been completely demolished and there was a huge hole in the middle of the road. Luckily no one in either of the houses had been killed, but everything they owned was destroyed. When it got light, we went down West Parade to see what we could do to help. The neighbours were all in the street. The bombs had landed very near the Suttons' and the Boswells' houses and all their windows were gone. Mrs Boswell, who always looked so elegant, had on an old coat and her face was smeared with soot. When we got back home I cried. It wasn't because of the damage. It was because Mrs Boswell's face was dirty.

After a few days the Water Board managed to set up a stand pipe in West Parade – so it was back to carrying water, as we had done at Eccles. And, since we couldn't flush the lavatory, the chamber pots came in useful. So did our paraffin cooking stove, because gas and electricity took longer to be connected.

Everyone was determined to carry on as usual. Our neighbour Mr Sutton was a very keen gardener, and after the raid his garden was completely covered with earth and debris from the bomb that had fallen next door. Within two days it was immaculate again. He had cleared it and planted new plants in record time – just to show Hitler he couldn't win. A shop near West Parade had had all its windows shattered by the blast from the bombs. People didn't swear much in those days, but next day the shop was open for business with a big notice: 'We're blasted well open.'

Somerleyton Street near West Parade

Two nights later 29th April, there was another enormous raid. This time we managed to get to the shelter in time, together with the Osbornes – and my father was there, which meant it didn't seem so bad.

When we explored Norwich after the two raids, we found that whole streets of houses had been destroyed. The shop where we bought our school uniforms wasn't there any more. Curls, one of the department stores where my mother and her friends used to have morning coffee, was just a hole in the ground, and another, Buntings, had had its roof blown off.

We found out later that over 200 people were killed and 700 had been injured in those raids, and three of the thirty-six medieval churches in Norwich were destroyed. But they didn't get the cathedral.

(Years later I learnt that more than 30,000 houses and nearly 1,000 offices and factories in Norwich were damaged or destroyed during the war.)

After the second big raid a lot of people decided it was not safe to sleep in Norwich any more. My father contacted a farmer in Tasburgh about 10 miles from Norwich and asked if we could sleep there. We were lucky to have a car and petrol to put in it. As we drove, we passed lots of families, carrying bundles of clothes and bedding, walking out of the city to sleep in the fields.

Today Tasburgh is virtually a suburb of Norwich; then it was in the depths of the country. There was no electricity and the house was lit by oil lamps. The lavatory was an earth closet in an outdoor shed. I slept in a feather bed – a great soft mattress entirely filled with feathers. There was a big solid-fuel cooker and a new-born piglet, the runt of the litter, was wrapped in a blanket and put in the bottom oven of the Aga to keep warm. Nothing seemed to have changed for centuries. After a few nights we decided it was safe to go back and sleep at home.

Two months after the Blitz there was another huge raid, with incendiary bombs as well as high explosives. Incendiary bombs burst into flames when they land.

This was the raid when St Julian's church, where Julian of Norwich lived, was badly damaged. But although Julian was to mean so much to me later on, in those days I had not even heard of her.

So many incendiaries fell on the roof of the cathedral that it melted the lead – but the firemen and the firewatchers managed to put them out. One incendiary bomb fell through the roof of Dr Muriel's house next door. Miss Muriel scooped it up with a long-handled shovel, threw it outside and put it out with her stirrup pump. Nothing got the better of her.

St Julian's church after the raid

During one of these raids our laundry was bombed. I've told you how some things were always sent to the laundry. It just so happened that, on that particular week, my mother, who had no one to help her with the washing any more, had sent an extra lot of things – not only sheets, pillowcases, table cloths and shirts (lots of them) but towels, tea towels, pyjamas and underwear as well. Nothing came back. We had to make the few remaining things last as long as possible.

When the sheets got thin we cut them in half and turned them 'sides to middle'. This meant you had an uncomfortable seam to lie on. Eventually they got holes in them – I still remember getting my toes twiddled up in the holes in the sheets at the bottom of the bed.

CHAPTER 19

Ring Out Wild Bells

It wasn't just the sheets that wore into holes. Our clothes were pretty threadbare, too. Replacing them was difficult because, like food, they were rationed. We had books of clothing coupons, and had to hand over a certain number when you bought each item. Fortunately Mr and Miss Bryant who lived in West Parade – you remember I told you he called his business 'Francois' – were sometimes not too fussy about getting the exact number of coupons. The dress my mother is wearing in the photograph taken in 1942 came from there, and so did Rosalind's. I'm wearing a hand-me-down with puff sleeves (ugh!) and a soppy collar.

But there was not a lot to buy in any case. Once the word got around that a shop had got some stock, there were lengthy queues (I remember queuing for hours and getting a wonderful pair of red Joyce shoes) and the queues for nylon stockings were enormous. I needed new clothes because I grew out of them – but of course there was always a supply of my sisters' outgrown clothes. I also wore their outgrown shoes, which weren't very comfortable. Everybody had to 'make do and mend.' I don't think people mend clothes these days. They just throw them away.

We used to make our own clothes out of any material we could find, and we sometimes cut up old dresses and made a new dress out of two old ones. It became fashionable to have two different patterns of material in one dress. Miss Muriel found a khaki nylon parachute on her roof, which I think had been used to drop the incendiary bomb she had scooped up with her shovel. She gave it to Thelma, who made it into a petticoat.

We had to 'make do' with food, too. Because I was a child, food rationing did not really concern me. I just ate what food was there. But for my mother it must have been a nightmare. All I remember for sure is that the ration of butter was 2oz (50g) per person per week, which didn't go far, and the meat ration per person was what you could buy for one shilling and tuppence. (I can't really translate that because the value of money has changed such a lot, but it's not very much.) And there was dried egg powder and dried potatoes. George didn't deliver the groceries any more with his horse and cart, we couldn't use the car for shopping, and my mother had to carry home all the groceries and vegetables. The shopping was so heavy that she pulled a muscle in her arm and had to rub strange black ointment on it to try to make it better. Sometimes now, when I look round the huge variety of things in the supermarket, and all the lovely shiny cars in the car park, I think back and wonder if people realise how very fortunate we are.

Most of our food was grown in England but food we couldn't grow, or couldn't grow enough of – like sugar and wheat – was brought to us across the Atlantic from America by convoys of merchant ships, escorted by warships. The convoys were bombed and attacked by German aircraft and submarines. Because it was so dangerous only essential food was brought. There was no room for luxuries like oranges and lemons and bananas and grapes. Some children grew up not knowing what a banana looked like. There was even a song:

> Yes, we have no bananas!
> We have no bananas today!

The only fruit we had in those years were things we could grow at home – apples, pears and soft fruit like blackcurrants. This meant there was a risk of vitamin C deficiency and the Ministry of Food produced rose-hip syrup for children. There were no vitamin C tablets then. My friends and I used to cycle out and pick rosehips from the wild roses in the hedges (there were still a lot of hedges full of wild roses very near Norwich in those days). We got money for these, but I can't remember how the system worked.

Our bicycles were really useful. There was petrol rationing, and although my father had petrol for work, we could not use the car for pleasure. The coast was out of bounds, and there was nowhere to go for holidays. So at the weekends in summer sometimes we all used to go out into the country on our bicycles and take a picnic. Fortunately we knew our way about. At the beginning of the war all the signposts had been taken down so that, if German paratroops landed, they would not know where they were. *(I can't imagine they wouldn't have had maps, but I suppose every little helps.)*

Everything in Norwich looked rundown during the war. People were either in uniform, or shabbily dressed. The shops looked dismal. They had very little to sell. The glass in all the big display windows was taken out and a small window, which could be blacked out, left in the centre. The medieval stained glass in the east window of St Peter

Mancroft – the big church beside the market place – was taken away to be stored somewhere safe. One of my great joys was to see it put back again in all its glory when the war was over. Most buildings had sandbags piled round them. There were stirrup pumps and buckets of sand, to be used to put out fires, in every shop and office.

Soon there was war damage everywhere. Bombed sites were cordoned off. A big static water tank was put on one of them to be used to help fight fires. Houses were shabby. There was no paint to repaint them. Broken windows were boarded up. There was no glass to replace them. The public clocks stopped – there was no one to repair them. Building work stopped. The new City Hall in Norwich was almost finished. For years there were blank walls with steel girders sticking out of them showing where the rest of the building would have been.

Everything looked shabby at home, too. We didn't have crisp white tablecloths any more, and the silver that Irene and I used to polish got tarnished and was put away. Now that my sisters were working and my mother busy with the Red Cross, it seemed strange to come home to an empty house, but my dog was there to welcome me, and I felt very important as I pulled the blackout curtains and lit the fire my father had laid ready, so that the house would be warm when the others came home.

You must wonder how we amused ourselves with no television, no DVDs and no computer games, but you don't miss what you have never had. We sometimes went to the cinema – finding our way there and back in the blackout and hoping there would not be an air raid – and I remember laughing a lot at the *Road To...* films with Bob Hope, Bing Crosby and Dorothy Lamour. My sister Rosalind was very keen on Deanna Durbin and she went to her films with Daisy Osborne, and took me with them. (I'd stopped taking refuge under the seat by this time!)

Nowadays cinemas are split up into several different screens, so you have a choice of several films. In my day there was one film shown in one big auditorium. What I remember most about it is the smell. I don't think there was much ventilation (there certainly wasn't air-conditioning). Nearly everyone smoked, and there was an ash tray on the back of each seat. I don't think these were emptied often and the place reeked of stale cigarettes. You could see the smoke curling up in the light coming from the projector at the back of the hall. It was fashionable to smoke in those days and nobody realised it could give you cancer – even if you were just breathing smoke from other people's cigarettes.

The theatre was still open and we saw *The Man Who Came To Dinner* and *Arsenic and Old Lace* – and the ballet still came to Norwich. There were War Charities concerts (a choir of American airmen sang in one, and in another I was a baby clown and danced with a pantomime horse).

Coal was rationed – like everything else – and we only had enough to keep a fire in the dining room, so we brought in comfortable chairs and sat round the fire there. Once a week there was a radio programme called ITMA (everything was called by its initials during the war and ITMA was short for It's That Man Again) which we thought extremely funny, and we read – and of course we played all the games we used to play at Eccles, like Monopoly and card games. And on a lot of evenings we used to sing.

It may seem strange to count singing as a pastime, but in my mother's day (which wasn't just before television, but before radio and cinema) it was quite usual to invite friends round for a 'musical evening' – and we just went back to the old ways. Both my sisters played the piano, so we would ask friends round, get out the sheet music and sing. Rosalind had left school and was working in an office. She and her great friend 'Woolly' were so keen on singing they used to cycle home at lunchtime to practise. They planned to be opera singers after the war, or film stars like Deanna Durbin. My father never sang (I think he must have been tone deaf) so it was a great treat, when one of the ARP messengers came round, to have a male voice instead of just sopranos and contraltos. Singing together doesn't just make music, it does more than that. I've read about a choir in Sydney, formed from homeless people, who have found that singing together has made all the difference to their lives. And soldiers sing marching songs to keep their spirits up.

We used to sing a couple of these – 'Pack up your troubles in your old kit bag' and 'It's a long way to Tipperary' – but I had no idea they were First World War songs. We also sang some of the new wartime songs – 'We're going to hang out our washing on the Siegfried Line' and 'There'll always be an England'. Then there were songs from Deanna Durbin's films, arias from operas, parts of Handel's *Messiah*, Negro spirituals, Gilbert and Sullivan, and a strange one from my mother's childhood called *Excelsior*.

It might sound a dreary life, but what kept our spirits up was the knowledge that, even if you were only a child, everything you did was important. It mattered if you checked the blackout to make sure no chink of light was showing; it mattered if you switched off lights to save electricity; it mattered if you grew vegetables instead of flowers – and it mattered if you only had five inches of water in your bath. We knew that the King and Queen had had a line painted on their bath in Buckingham Palace to make sure it wasn't filled above five inches. We were all in the war together.

We took our spare aluminium saucepans to be melted down – they went to make Spitfires. Bins were put in every street for waste food – potato peelings and such like. It went to make pig food. The iron railings round the parks and people's gardens were taken away. They were melted down for tanks and guns. We knew that everything we did helped the war effort and brought victory nearer.

This photo is us in June 1942.

At school we had to use every scrap of paper in our exercise books before we were allowed a new one. And in the needlework class at Lonsdale House, instead of doing embroidery, we knitted sea boot stockings out of oiled wool for sailors. (I wonder if they ever wore them.)

The radio was our main source of amusement and information. It played lots of popular songs and there were variety shows and, of course, the news. Today television news brings you all the action as it happens. News in those days was censored, because we didn't want to give information to the enemy. The less *they* knew about what was going on, the better. (There were posters warning us that 'Careless Talk Costs Lives').

So when news bulletins reported raids, the announcers did not give the exact location where German bombs had been dropped. They often just said 'German bombs were dropped at random on southern England.' There was great hilarity when the German radio picked this up and reported: 'The town of Random was heavily bombed again last night.'

You might think that in these conditions we would be discouraged and terrified, but the threat to life made it all the more worth living. Winston Churchill's broadcasts summed up the spirit of the time. It's nearly seventy years since I heard them, but I shall always remember part of them. 'We shall fight on the beaches, we shall fight in the fields and in the streets....we shall never surrender.'

I've checked the date of this one, and find it was 4th June 1940 when I was nine years old. My parents listened in the drawing room, and I sat on the floor by the window. Afterwards we felt as though we had been given a great boost of strength. I shall also never forget another speech, a fortnight later: 'Let us so bear ourselves that if the British Empire lasts for a thousand years, men will still say: "This was their finest hour".'

You've studied this war as history, Madison, and so you will probably have listened to these speeches, but you have to think yourself back into the summer of 1940 to understand the effect they had on us. We knew that we were at the crossroads of history and that everything depended on us.

It was unimportant that we didn't have enough food, or clothes, or money; that our city was being bombed; that we had to run into the air raid shelter most nights. We knew that we were a million times better off than the people in France and Holland and Belgium and Poland

and Czechoslovakia. And we knew that, if we held out, as we were determined to do, then things would get better again for them, too.

And they did. On 8th May 1945 the Germans surrendered. We heard the news on the wireless. That evening we simply could not stay at home. We went out into the street and joined the hundreds of other people who were making their way to the market place in the centre of the city. No one organised it – we just felt we had to go there. When we got there we joined hands with people we didn't know, and we danced in the street. Someone would start up a song, and everyone else would join in. We formed lines and danced in and out of the traffic islands. Over the noise of all the jubilation was the sound of the bells of St Peter Mancroft, the big church beside the market place, ringing out a triumphal peal that seemed to go on and on.

Church bells had been silent all through the war because they were to be the warning signal if German paratroops had landed. They made up for it now. When you go to Norwich you'll see a board in the ringing chamber in the tower of St Peter Mancroft which tells you these same bells were rung for the victory over the Spanish Armada in 1588, for the victory at Trafalgar in 1805 and Waterloo in 1815. (There's also an enormous pewter jug for beer for the ringers. Bell-ringing goes on for hours and is thirsty work – just read Dorothy L. Sayers' detective story *The Nine Tailors* if you want to find out about it.)

So we danced in the streets and the bells pealed out. We took down the blackout – and the lights shone out again all over the world.

CHAPTER 20

French without Tears

By the time I danced in the streets, I had left Lonsdale House and gone to Norwich High School for Girls. I went there in April 1943, in the middle of the school year, when I was 12.

It had been started by the Girls Public Day School Trust in 1875 – just 68 years earlier – when education for girls was still a bit suspect. Today's feminists seem to take the credit for opening up careers for women. But they would not be in their jobs if it were not for the early pioneers of women's education who fought for girls to be allowed to sit the same exams as boys. It is they who are really responsible.

The High School charged fees, but they were very modest – about £36 ($75) a year, I think. The school was small compared with your school – about 400 girls – but it seemed big then. I had an interview with the maths teacher, who was glad to hear I knew about Pythagoras. Then I met the English teacher who asked me to write an essay on Tennyson's *Morte D'Arthur* – and I was accepted. Nowadays it's very hard to get in. You have to put your name down – practically at birth. When Aunt Lucy went there in the 1960s she had to take an entrance test at the age of four (and I had been careful to play lacrosse for the Old Girls, hoping it might help.) The fees in those days were still affordable – but now, since the abolition of the government direct grant, they're well over £8,000 (nearly $20,000) a year. It makes me very sad that only rich parents can afford to send their daughters there now, and angry, too, that the government should deliberately put this and other schools like it beyond the reach of most parents.

I used to cycle to school (and back home again for a meal) every day. It took ten minutes each way. I cycled winter and summer – rain, shine, sleet and snow – like most of the other girls. Hardly anyone came by car. You see why we had cloakrooms where we hung up our wet outdoor coats and changed our shoes. Nowadays there's too much traffic for children to cycle safely, and the 'school run' is part of life and causes traffic jams. Nobody goes home at midday now, and schools are expected to provide meals as part of their job.

The school day began with Prayers – a hymn, a bible reading, another hymn, followed by notices. The whole school assembled in the gym. Four hundred girls got from their classrooms to the gym in total silence in about four minutes – which was quite an achievement.

The High School, like Lonsdale House, was in what had once been a private house. It was a very grand one, set in its own grounds with plenty of room for tennis courts and playing fields. An assembly hall – which doubled as a gym – had been built on to it, plus extra form-rooms and two science laboratories. Science was a new experience for me. There were Bunsen burners and test tubes and litmus paper and all sorts of interesting experiments – like blowing a flame through a blow-pipe at mercury powder and making lots of little silver balls that rushed about all over the bench. But the day I had to cut up a bull's eye – a real one from the butcher, not a sweet from Mr Clements' shop – I realised I was never going to make a scientist.

French was a different proposition. It seemed a useful thing to be able to do, since there were a lot of French people – including Free French soldiers – in Norwich after the fall of France. Going to France to practise our French was not an option just then. We should have been arrested or shot if we'd landed – possibly both. Two people taught French – Miss Moroni and Mrs Smythe. Both of them seemed exotic, each in their different ways. Miss Moroni was exotic because she was foreign – half Italian and half French. Certainly the way she spoke French didn't sound the same as the way they spoke it at Lonsdale House. She was very tall and dark, and I don't think she got on too well with the other members of staff. This was rather good for our education, since she would come sweeping into the classroom and complain about them in very fast French. This was so interesting that we soon learnt to understand what she was saying. But we also learnt lots of French irregular verbs and sang jolly French songs – which is very good for pronunciation.

Mrs Smythe was exotic for different reasons – she was very pretty, she wore wonderful clothes (the other staff didn't seem to care much about fashion and wore shapeless woolly cardigans) and she was married. *(Most of your teachers, men and women, are married, Madison, but in my day Mrs Smythe was the only married teacher on the staff.)*

There were no men on the staff. This was lucky for us. Girls were much better taught than boys during the war. If you talk to men of my age you will find that, because all able-bodied men were called up, boys were taught by a motley collection of retired teachers – and men who had only one arm or leg, or could hardly see.

One reason for the lack of married women on the staff, though I didn't realise it at the time, was another war, from 1914 to 1918. Many of the women who taught me when I arrived at the High School must have been in their forties. Thousands of young men the right age to be their husbands had been killed on the battlefields some twenty-five years earlier. But that wasn't the only reason for there being so few married women. If one of them had married she would probably have given up teaching. A lot of women at that time didn't think it right to go on working once they were married, unless they needed the money.

I have a feeling Mrs Smythe might have needed the money. She was married to an artist, and they – notoriously - tend to starve in garrets. The Smythes didn't live in a garret, but in a little house beside the Maddermarket Theatre (more about this later) where Paul Smythe's job was painting scenery. All this made Mrs Smythe seem even more exotic.

Several of the teachers, among them Miss Moroni, still lived at home with a widowed mother. But some of them had had to move away from their families to get a job. So while single men were still lodgers in other people's houses, these single women were far more independent. They were capable of earning a living and running households of their own. Some shared a house with another teacher. One or two of them even had their own cars – an Austin 7 was popular – and the rest lived near enough to walk or cycle. Miss Moroni pedalled to school, majestically, on a tall upright bicycle, not like today when a lot of the pupils at your school now arrive by car, as well as the staff.

(One strange thing I discovered later, when I was editing a history of the school, was that because student numbers virtually halved at the beginning of the war, all the staff were sacked. They were then re-appointed on a term-by-term basis. Numbers did pick up, and no one had to go, but the staff were later warned that their salaries might be reduced. I don't think this could happen today.)

We took School Certificate in English, French, History, Geography, Latin or German, Maths, Physics, and Chemistry. We had to do at least five subjects and were not allowed to do more than eight. You were only allowed to do Art and Religious Knowledge if your other subjects were a bit shaky. This was because unless you got at least five subjects you failed the whole Certificate. *(Although in Australia you still have School Certificate and Higher School Certificate, in England they have been replaced by O levels and A levels and you can take as few subjects as you like at any one time. In my day it was still called the School Leaving Certificate and very few people stayed on at school after that.)*

Teaching was very formal. We sat in rows at desks. The teacher sat at a high desk in front of the class, and behind her was a blackboard, which she would write on with chalk and rub out with a special rubber. It seems very primitive compared with the electronic whiteboards you have today, where the writing disappears at the touch of a button and can be printed off afterwards.

Although we had a physics laboratory and a chemistry laboratory, we didn't have anything called a language laboratory. There were no tape recorders and the only way we heard French and German was spoken by real people. And of course we didn't have computers, and the internet didn't exist. If we wanted extra information we had to look it up in a book – and even books were few and far between during the war because of the paper shortage.

I often used to go to the public library to study in the holidays. There was no multimedia, no CDs or DVDs or photographs – just books. The books I wanted were mostly in the reference section and couldn't be taken away.

There were never very many people there, but there were usually two or three old men who seemed to spend all morning looking at a book without turning the pages. They often fell asleep or started muttering. I have a feeling they went there to keep out the cold.

I had a few reference books at home. One of my treasured books in those days was *The Oxford Companion to English Literature*, and my copy has become dog-eared over the years. But now I hardly open it, nor my *Encyclopaedia Britannica* – which was such a prized possession when I managed to buy a secondhand copy years later – because, like you I get nearly all my information from the internet.

(Much as I appreciate the internet, I sometimes think, because so much is available so easily, that you don't retain the information, but it goes in one ear and out the other. And for English literature there's such a huge number of 'study aids' that I imagine you could pass exams without even having read the books if you were lazy enough.)

In geography lessons there were no films to show us what other countries were like, and of course there was no chance of travelling to any of them. And overhead projectors and Power Point hadn't been invented. Instead we had a globe that pulled down from the ceiling, and something called an epidiascope. This was a machine that could project a picture in a book onto a screen at the front of the room. Blinds had to be drawn over the windows when this was used, so that the room was in darkness. This is one reason my geography is a little shaky. While I am not too bad on such things as igneous and sedimentary rocks, I was born without a sense of direction and without the ability (which seems to go with it) to read a map – which is a disadvantage when you are learning geography. But there was one thing in which I excelled. While the room was darkened for the epidiascope, there was a competition to see who could crawl the most times from one side of the room to the other without attracting attention. I was good at that.

Our history lessons would have been very different from yours because we didn't learn any Australian history, just British and European. There's an awful lot of it – the Norman Conquest, Henry VIII and the dissolution of the monasteries, Queen Elizabeth, the Spanish Armada, the Stuarts, Cromwell, the Glorious Revolution – and that's before you get to the American War of Independence, the French Revolution, Napoleon, Trafalgar and Waterloo. And there's lots more besides. We certainly would not have learnt the history of the Second World War, as you do, because we were living through it. We would have been amazed to think that it would count as 'history'.

I enjoyed all the subjects (apart from cutting up bull's eyes) including maths. Algebra and geometry were fine but I get numbers muddled up, and so I often make silly mistakes in arithmetic. In year 9 (aged 14) there was one ghastly sum. First I must tell you that there are twelve pence in a shilling and twenty shillings in a pound sterling. Then there are 112 pounds weight (written 112 lb) in a hundredweight (written cwt). We had learnt all these weights and measures by heart a long time ago.

The sum went: 'A grocer buys 2 cwt of tea at £10 17s. 6d a cwt and 3 cwt of tea at £12 13s. a cwt. He mixes them and sells them at 5s. 6d per lb. What is his percentage profit? There's a lot of room for error in that if you don't have a calculator.

I expect the sport you enjoy most is swimming, Madison. That wasn't an option for us. We couldn't go to the sea any more, and both the two public swimming pools in Norwich had been closed. One of them, the Samson and Hercules, had been turned into a dance hall – and was one of the places where my parents hoped my sister wouldn't meet American airmen. None of the schools had its own swimming pool. We didn't do athletics because we didn't have a track. We just had a Sports Day with races and high jump.

(*Now the school has an athletics track, sports hall, gym, a drama studio, theatre, and a swimming pool, nearly all of it paid for by fund-raising by parents and pupils in the school.*)

In summer we played tennis. In those days there were just two hard courts and eight grass courts. The school had been one of the first to start playing tennis. (Did you know lawn tennis didn't begin until 1877 – twenty-two years after the school was started?) Our racquets were made of laminated wood, not metal, like yours. The handles were longer and the hitting area was smaller. (*I saw one in a museum the other day, which shook me.*) Another thing I notice is that the standard of tennis-playing has changed out of recognition over the years. In those days the best school players might have survived a game or two at Wimbledon. Now it would be complete annihilation.

In the early days the school had played hockey, but by the time I arrived the winter game was lacrosse. Everyone else in my year had been learning this for a year, so I had to catch up. I used to turn up at school at 8.30 instead of 9 and practise with my friends before school.

It's a wonderful game, Madison. I played it with great enjoyment for the next 25 years. We were all very keen and we finally achieved our ambition – the School Team.

The other great goal was the School Play, which Mrs Smythe used to produce. Getting a part in this was another ambition. Mrs Smythe also acted herself, at a theatre called the Maddermarket, and was very talented. I'm not sure that the theatre plays a great part in your life, Madison, but the Maddermarket played such a big part in mine, that I'm going to tell you about it.

CHAPTER 21

The Freedom of the City

The Maddermarket Theatre was run by an Irish actor called Nugent Monck, who had transformed an old warehouse into an Elizabethan theatre. This might not seem remarkable these days, now that Shakespeare's Globe Theatre has been rebuilt at Southwark, but back then it was extraordinary. Modern theatres are designed so that plays can be put on in the round, and lighting can come from all over the auditorium. But in those days the stage in all theatres was set back behind an arch with a curtain in front. The curtain went up, and the play was performed as if it were a picture in a frame.

But in an Elizabethan theatre the front part of the stage, called an 'apron', jutted out into the audience. There as an inner recess at the back of the stage with a balcony above it – think of *Romeo and Juliet* – which gives endless possibilities. Of course commercial theatres have to make a profit *(there were no government grants for the Arts in those days)* and they cost a lot to run and have a lot of seats to fill. So this meant the plays in the Theatre Royal in Norwich were not very adventurous – though I'd much enjoyed *The Man who came to Dinner* and *Arsenic and Old Lace* when they came on tour.

But the Maddermarket was small and so were the bills – so Nugent Monck could afford to put on plays that did not have to attract large audiences. What made the bills even smaller was that the actors didn't have to be paid. They were all amateurs. *(I expect Mrs Smythe's husband, Paul, was paid for painting scenery, or perhaps he just got the little house instead.)* Amateur actors can be very good indeed, some of them as good as professionals. But the great drawback about amateurs is that the publicity sometimes goes to their heads, and they begin to put on airs – and that's disastrous. Nugent Monck knew all about this pitfall. He made it a rule that there were no names in the programmes, and there were no curtain calls. And the acting was superb.

There was only one way to see Shakespeare and other classic plays in those days, and that was to see them live. None of Shakespeare's plays had been filmed until Laurence Olivier's Henry V in 1945. It was a sensation. We all rushed off to see it. Now you can pick up a DVD of virtually all Shakespeare's plays and view them at home at your leisure.

There was only one play a month at the Maddermarket – except in August – and I went to nearly all of them. Plays are meant to be acted, not read, and to see so many of them brought to life was thrilling. There were plays by Shakespeare (lots), Shaw, Molière, Oscar Wilde, Chekhov, Sheridan, Racine – and there was Greek tragedy and Restoration comedy, and lots more besides. The seats at the Maddermarket didn't cost very much. One or two of them were behind the pillars that held up the roof, so you had to crane your neck round them to see the stage. These cost even less – one shilling and sixpence – which suited me. But the Maddermarket was only one of the interesting places in Norwich.

When I started this story, I was just a small child being taken everywhere by my mother. But by now I'm able to go to places on my own. I had coffee with my own friends instead of my mother's. Norwich was a wonderful city to grow up in, and it was perfectly safe for children to explore it by themselves. It was still like that when your father Oliver and Auntie Lucy were growing up in the 1960s and 70s. When we lived in the Cathedral Close they could walk all over the city by themselves from the time they were about six or seven. Nowadays I don't think children would be allowed to.

I got to know the Cathedral well during the twenty years we

lived in the Close. Your father got to know it very well, too. He went there every morning for School Assembly. But I first got to know it when I explored it on my own as a child. In those days it seemed to me even bigger than it does today – huge and cool and holy. But the first time I saw it, the stonework was black from centuries of grime and candle-smoke, not a glorious creamy white as it is today.

One of the places I liked best was the cloisters, where the roof bosses had just been repainted. King George V and Queen Mary came to Norwich for the reopening of the cloisters but, not many weeks before they were due to arrive, the cathedral organ caught fire. The mess was so horrendous that all the stonework in the cathedral had to be cleaned – and cleaned in a hurry before they arrived – which turned out to be a blessing in disguise.

There are literally hundreds of roof bosses – big stones at the joints of the vaulting – in the cloisters, nearly all of them carved with scenes from the Bible. Looking up at them is a neck-aching business, and there were trolleys with mirrored tops that you could push round the cloisters to look at them.

(There aren't just mirrored trolleys now, but inter-active videos to explore the cloisters and the nave roof bosses, too, which are even more magnificent. I especially liked Noah and his Ark.)

When I left the Cathedral I'd cross the road, go past the Maid's Head Hotel (one of the many places that can claim 'Queen Elizabeth I slept here') and walk up Elm Hill, which is a complete street of medieval houses.

In my day Elm Hill was rather run down and scruffy. Not many years before, in the early 1930s, it was so dilapidated that the City Council was debating if the expense of restoring it was justified, or whether to pull it down. It was only the Lord Mayor's casting vote that saved it from being demolished – the fate of a lot of medieval streets in Norwich, which had degenerated into slums, in the 1920s and 1930s.

In 1928 a Mr Day wrote to the Eastern Daily Press:

'Is not Elm Hill, with its ugly old tumbledown buildings, which remind us of how fever-pestered our forefathers were, very ugly...Some of the old workshops are simply little fever-dens for any poor working man who may be obliged to toil there. I have been in more than one, and the stuffy air was just what killed out forefathers off at an early age...Elm Hill is the most shameful spot in a decent city. As if a decent citizen would be proud to walk about in his grandfather's worn-out breeches!'

It's easy to laugh at Mr Day, but he had a point. Epidemics of 'fever' – the general name for cholera, typhoid and influenza - were still common in England. The houses in Elm Hill still had earth closets instead of  flushing lavatories, and they got their water from a pump at the top of the street, just below the graveyard of St Peter Hungate church.

Some houses were barely habitable. A former landlord of the Adam and Eve, the oldest pub in Norwich, told me that when he lived in Elm Hill in the 1920s – you can see the house in the picture, it was over the Dog Market – the roof leaked, the house was overrun by rats, and there was a huge hole in the staircase where two treads were missing.

(You'll know that in Australia the same arguments – that the place was unsightly and insanitary – were used in 1968 for a scheme to bulldoze the entire area of the Rocks in Sydney. The Sydney Cove Redevelopment Authority was authorised to move everyone out and replace the narrow lanes and little houses with huge high-rise towers of offices and multi-storey car parks. But the people who lived in the Rocks fought back. They did not want their homes pulled down. The Trade Unions backed them, and refused to work on the scheme. The battle raged for years – and there were street scuffles and dozens of arrests. Finally the planners backed down. The Rocks is so beautiful that today it seems incredible that anyone wanted to pull it down. But not many people live there any more and, like Elm Hill, it has become a tourist show-piece.)

My favourite shop in Elm Hill was a second-hand bookshop. Outside were green Penguin detective stories at sixpence each. Inside the shop, the books were floor-to-ceiling. I've still got the leather-bound Victorian editions of poetry I bought there. When you'd chosen your books, you knocked at the glass-panelled door at the back of the shop and Mr Higgins, who lived behind the shop, came out and took your money. *(I still haunt second-hand bookshops, as you know, since you've had to drag me out of so many in Sydney.)*

On the other side of the road, in an upstairs room, was Miss Tinkler's Dancing School, where, like you, when I was very small, I used to learn ballet. Elm Hill is paved with flint cobblestones, and my mother used to find it difficult to walk along it in her high heels.

Further along was a shop that sold carriage clocks. Next to that was a little shop that sold puppies and kittens, where I spent a lot of time looking in the window. And opposite was a shop that sold paintings. It was full of big dark canvasses on easels – and it was owned by Stella Nightingale's father. *(You'll remember she taught us riding.)* There always seemed to be a lot of men in there talking, and I never dared go in.

Opposite his shop there was a pub called the Briton's Arms, which smelt of beer and was rather disreputable. *(I've got a painting of it by a friend of mine, which he did when he was at Norwich Art School in 1928. He painted it sitting outside Mr Nightingale's shop and told me that, while he was painting, a lot of drunken men came out of the pub and threw beer bottles at him.)* Elm Hill isn't scruffy any more. It's a Tourist Attraction and is full of shops selling things nobody needs.

Once I got to the top of Elm Hill it was just a short walk to Castle Meadow. And there, high on its hill, was the Norman Castle. There aren't many hills in Norfolk so, when the Normans came, they had to build one specially to put their castle on. In the 1800s it had been used as a jail, but it was a museum now, and I'd climb up the steep steps among the cow parsley and go in through the turnstiles.

Nearly everything in the Castle Museum was in a glass case. There were lots of stuffed animals – lions, tigers, polar bears – many of which had been shot by local gentry.

(It might seem strange to have stuffed animals in a museum, but there were no zoos nearby, and I suppose this was the only way to show people what they looked like. Nowadays everyone knows all about them through wildlife programmes on television.)

There were cases of wild birds (also shot by local gentry). The wild-fowlers had been so successful that a lot of species had been wiped out. A card beside a stuffed bittern read sombrely: NOW EXTINCT. *(Fortunately they've now been re-established and at night on the Broads you can hear their strange booming sound once more.)* There were glass cases of butterflies and birds' eggs. And there was a rather grisly panorama showing Ancient Britons working in local flint mines.

Even more grisly were the dungeons. The walls were covered with graffiti carved into the walls by men who had been chained there in the darkness.

But just walking about Norwich was exciting. Like most modern cities Sydney is laid out on a grid pattern – but the streets of Norwich were traced out centuries ago by the paths people used to tread, and full of unexpected lanes and alleys. Down one you might find an Elizabethan house. In another there would be a thatched cottage. When you had coffee in the Curate House or Suckling House, you found yourself in a Tudor mansion. And on almost every corner there was a medieval church and you could push open the door and explore.

Right in the centre of Norwich is the market place. The market used to be outside the Cathedral Close but, when the Normans came, they moved it nearer their Castle so they could keep an eye on what went on. It's still there and you can buy almost anything – eggs, vegetables, fruit, fish, flowers, meat, china, clocks, batteries, books, brooms, dresses, jeans, saucy underwear, suitcases, scent, shoes... And if you get hungry you can get hot pies and hamburgers and fish and chips – or cockles and winkles and whelks which are served on little white saucers.

At the back of the market in my day, on Saturdays, was a stall run by Alf the Purse King. He didn't just sell handbags – he put on a performance. *(I've heard this sort of thing from 'barkers' in cut-price shops in Sydney.)* He'd start off 'spruiking' (a word I've learnt from you) a handbag at fifteen pounds, and finally sell it for a fiver. And a little further along there'd be the Salvation Army Band playing rousing hymns. But these were only two of the attractions in Norwich on Saturday.

The biggest and best was the Cattle Market.

You don't meet many cows walking along the streets of Sydney – though hundreds of cattle come in every year for the Easter Show – but in Norwich on a Saturday the country came into the city.

The Cattle Market was in the centre of Norwich, right beside the Castle, and cattle, and sheep, and pigs, and goats, and horses, and poultry, and rabbits, were all brought there to be sold. Lots of cattle came by train. The cattle trucks were unloaded at Trowse, about a mile from the Cattle Market, and the cows were driven along King Street to the market. When I say 'driven' I don't mean put into a motor lorry. They walked – with a man with a stick, a boy and a dog walking behind them to keep them going in the right direction.

There was a lot of noise and shouting – and smells. And a great deal of muck underfoot. Sometimes a pig or a calf would break loose and be recaptured. And the farmers would all be there, leaning on the rails and eyeing the livestock with a knowledgeable eye. The pubs all round the market would do a roaring trade. You remember that Mr Boston, who lived in West Parade, had his pawnbroker's shop just by the market. I expect Saturday was his busiest day.

The horses were auctioned separately, beside a church called St John Timberhill. This was my favourite place. The auctioneer would read out a description: 'Six-year-old bay gelding, 14 hands, quiet to ride and drive.' One of the men would shout 'Mind your backs!' and, with his long overall flapping, he'd run up and down to make the horse trot out. When there were no more bids, the auctioneer would bang his hammer down, and the horse was sold. I didn't think he was as good at selling as Alf the Purse King.

More than anything else, I wanted a pony of my own, and I sometimes wondered, if I had the money, what would happen if I bought one, took it home, and asked my parents if I could keep it in the garden. *(Years later I got my wish when I bought a pony – for Lucy, not for me – and we kept it in our garden in the Cathedral Close.)*

When you go to Norwich, Madison, you won't find sheep and cows in the streets any more. The livestock has been banished to a dreary place on the outskirts of Norwich. The site of the Cattle Market is a shopping mall, and the last I heard of Mr Boston's shop, it had been turned into a trendy restaurant. But just now I think it is time to leave the market, and get back to school, where there's a lot of work waiting to be done.

CHAPTER 22

Love and Money

But before we plunge back into school and working for exams, you must be wondering why so far I haven't said anything at all about two very important subjects – money and sex. The fact is that in those days we didn't have a lot of either.

Take money first. Some of my friends had pocket money given to them each week by their parents. It's hard to work out what the value of it would be in today's terms, but it didn't buy much. They could also earn a bit more by doing odd jobs – such as washing up or mowing the lawn. I didn't have any pocket money, because my parents reckoned I didn't need it because they would give me the money for the things I wanted. I think this was a mistake, because it is fun to make choices and to save up for things.

(I can't remember whether you had pocket money, but you hardly needed it because you've been able to earn quite a lot by minding friends' children and baby-sitting, and when you got older by working in coffee bars. And your friends who work on the checkout at supermarkets earn quite a lot of money.)

There were hardly any paid jobs for schoolchildren in my time, and none of my friends or I ever had a paid job. We weren't expected to. We couldn't have worked in a coffee bar because there weren't any. In England they didn't open until the 1950s when the first Espresso coffee machines were imported from Italy. Shops were only open from 9 to 5, five and a half days a week and so they had regular staff and didn't need shift-workers. And there were no baby-sitters, because either the family had a living-in maid, or there were lots of relations nearby who could take charge.

The only paid work was at Christmas when some of my friends would work at the General Post Office helping to sort mail.

This didn't matter because we didn't need much money. We didn't need money to buy clothes. There were no 'must-have' fashionable clothes we were longing for. Clothes for small children and for grown-ups were very different from each other – unlike today – and there was nothing to bridge the gap between them. The shops had departments labelled 'Maids' and 'Youths' which sold dreadful dreary clothes which our parents bought for us. There were no video games, or CDs, or DVDs, or iPods for us to spend our money on. There were no discos, and no mobile phones or the bills that go with them. About the only thing we needed money for was the cinema. It didn't cost much and we didn't go very often.

The fact that we had hardly any money explains the surprising fact that I was never a teenager. That doesn't mean that I missed out a few years and jumped from twelve to twenty. The word 'teenager' didn't exist. A 'teenager' identifies a marketing target. And it wasn't until children in their teens acquired spending power that the word came into widespread use (I'm guessing it was around the early 1960s.) You may think this sounds cynical, but I worked for years as advertising copywriter and I know what I'm talking about.

When I talked earlier about television, and the fact that we did not have it, I was thinking about the programmes. But it's also the advertising on television that has made your life and mine so different. *(I was working in an advertising agency when commercial television began in 1955. The first advertisement ever shown was one of ours – a tube of toothpaste embedded in an ice block, floating jerkily down a mountain stream. It was unfortunate that this was followed by a broadcast of a prize fight, and the next thing the viewer saw was a boxer spitting into a bucket.)*

And of course advertising isn't just on television. All of us are bombarded every day of our lives with a whole barrage of advertisements in magazines, junk mail and on the internet. And so another big difference between your life and mine is that, when I was growing up, we were encouraged to want less and less, while today people are encouraged to want more and more. During the war we were told to 'Make do and mend' – not spend, spend, spend.

George Herbert wrote in the 1600s:

I am content with what I have
Little be it or much
And, Lord, contentment still I crave
Because thou savest such.

But, wise as this advice is, being content with what you have doesn't make the wheels of industry go round. For most of my teenage years the wheels of industry were going round as fast as they could, making guns and ships and aeroplanes and tanks. Even when the war was over we weren't encouraged to spend, because nearly everything had to be exported to pay for the war. I remember a joke:

But once the post-war shortages were over, it was time to boost consumer demand. And for the first time 'teenagers' were targeted as a part of the market.

All age groups are targets, of course, not just teenagers. *(Now I am in my seventies they are trying to sell me stair lifts, hearing aids, retirement homes and, looking even further ahead, pre-paid funerals.)* But I like to think advertising doesn't have so much effect on me these days because, as you get older, you don't care so much about wearing the right clothes, or what people think of you. Do you know that wonderful poem of Jenny Joseph's:

> *When I am an old woman I shall wear purple*
> *With a red hat that doesn't go and doesn't suit me...*

Finishing up
> *...And make up for the sobriety of my youth.*

My youth was certainly a time of sobriety. I never went into a pub until after I had left school, and as far as I know my mother never went into one in her entire life. When we went out for a drive (before the war when we still had petrol) my father would usually stop at a pub and he would bring us out a tray of soft drinks. (We used to say our car couldn't pass the Ingham Swan, on the way to Eccles.) Then he'd go back in for a pint of beer. Then, as now children were not allowed in pubs, but my mother stayed in the car because very few women went into pubs in those days. *(I'm told that at that time in Australia women were not allowed to go into pubs except in the Ladies Bar, so that if a husband and wife went out together they would have to drink in separate bars.)*

At home there was a bottle of whisky nobody ever seemed to drink, and bottled beer for my father. My mother sometimes had a glass of sherry and got a bit giggly before Sunday lunch. People drink a lot more now than we did then. Pubs are open far longer hours – they used to close at 10 pm – and they make women customers feel welcome. Some are specially designed to attract young drinkers. There was no point in targeting young people in my day. We didn't have any money to spend – and so there was no point in designing alco-pops to please young palates, either.

Another big difference is that there were no available drugs. I know *(not from experience, but from the vintage detective stories I read)* that cocaine was fashionable and available in the 1930s. But it was very expensive, and only rich people could afford it. Cheaper drugs had not been invented, and no one was trying to sell 'pot' or 'ecstasy' to teenage girls and boys.

I didn't meet many boys when I was growing up because the schools in Norwich were all single-sex. Some of my friends had brothers, but either they were older and we were beneath their notice, or younger and they were beneath ours. We didn't mind. Boys and girls have different interests and we were quite happy with our girl friends. It was only when we were in the Sixth Form (Years 11 and 12 in Australia) that we started to meet boys in the Inter-Sixth Form Debating Society.

We enjoyed challenging each other in the debates, and began to make friends. We also got a glimpse of a different outlook. I was surprised to find that one pretty girl was very popular and that the boys didn't seem to care that she was hopeless at maths. If I'd realised this earlier I might have spent more time curling my hair and less on French irregular verbs – which is perhaps why single-sex girls schools are always top in the exam results league. We formed real friendships, too, just as genuine as those with our girl friends. I still exchange Christmas cards with my first boy friend. We would meet in groups for coffee at weekends, and talk about books and films – but never did more than hold hands. We were a bit vague about what people called 'the facts of life' but it didn't bother us. Our expectation – and our hope – was that one day we would fall in love and marry, and find out. But that was a romantic dream a long way in the future.

Some of our ideas about romance came from magazines and the one I sometimes read was the *Girl's Own Paper*. It had fiction, fashion hints and news of film stars. The film star sometimes featured was the young singer Deanna Durbin, who was shown posing with her spaniel dog (there was no mention of her marriage, nor of her divorce in 1943). The problems in the agony column, as I recall, concerned embarrassment about spotty complexions, too small (or too large) breasts, and schoolgirl 'crushes' and jealousies.

In the Australian magazine *Girlfriend* I picked up when I was staying with you, one agony column letter read: 'I really want to try different sex positions with my BF (boy friend), but I'm really scared that he'll see everything down there. I don't want him to! I'm really

125

self-conscious! Is there anything I can do to make sex fun and good without him seeing it all?' *(The answer: Tell him how you feel and take it slowly. While total darkness is one option it can be difficult to navigate in. Try subtle lighting. We all look better with the lights low anyway.)*

The next page, with the heading: 'Boost your STI-Q', gives details of the symptoms and treatment of the Sexually Transmitted Infections, Chlamydia, gonorrhoea, genital warts, hepatitis and HIV. *Girlfriend* is aimed at 13-17-year-olds.

Sex education is a standard requirement in most schools now and it seems not unreasonable to suppose that, having been taught the mechanics of reproduction without being given any education that 'having sex' can have any value other than recreational, children will lose no time in putting theory into practise.

People don't talk to grandmothers about this, but it seems clear that nowadays, far from being discouraged, children are expected – by grown-ups as well as by their contemporaries – to be sexually active and to have 'multiple sexual partners'. And that, whereas we believed that love came first and sex later, there is now pressure on children to 'have sex' with whoever is available, as soon and as often as possible. Love and affection don't seem to come into it – let alone long-term commitment – an attitude that seems to me to reduce human beings to the level of rabbits and guinea pigs. (In my view, there's more to be learnt about the meaning of love from reading *Romeo and Juliet* or John Donne than from reading a sex manual.)

All this sexual activity is very profitable for the pharmaceutical companies. Sales of condoms must be booming, and the contraceptive pill is a marketing man's dream. The sale of most drugs depends on someone being ill. But imagine the sales of a product that, potentially, is taken every day by every woman of child-bearing age in every country in the entire world – particularly if the cost of the drug is generally paid for by the government.

In my day, when the age of majority was 21, a lot of trouble was taken to see that girls (political correctness had not yet decreed that we must be called 'young women') were protected from sexual adventures.

At college, where the age-range was 18-21, we had to sign out if we were going out for the evening, and sign in when we got back at night (though you could always circumvent this by not signing out in the first place). Male visitors had to leave by 6 pm and there were heavy bars on the downstairs windows to keep out intruders.

(The college is very much bigger now and co-educational. Recently I was sent a copy of the college magazine. In an account of the opening – by Princess Anne – of a new hall of residence, it remarked, in passing, that all the study bedrooms have double beds.)

You may think today's attitude to sex is better and more 'liberated' than ours, but you also have to take into account that it often has unintended consequences. You don't need me to point out that, as well as the risk of being infected with nasty diseases, a great many teenage girls are having babies – and many others are having abortions (illegal in my day). The fathers of these boys are often teenage boys who are not mature enough to help bring up a child – let alone earn money to support it. Nor do you need me to point out that people who are still children themselves don't make ideal parents –and that it is an uncomfortable fact that the pursuit of happiness does not always mean you capture it.

So another huge difference between your life and mine is that it was in nobody's interest to sell me things or to encourage me to take drugs, or to get drunk, or to 'have sex'. And I'm extremely grateful.

CHAPTER 23

Hail Caesar!

We're nearing the end of the story of my first eighteen years. All that's left is the last two of them. As I told you, in those days it was unusual to stay on after School Certificate – called O levels today. Of the sixty girls in my year only about twelve stayed on. About half of these left after a year to do a secretarial course. I told you how difficult it was to work those old-fashioned typewriters. They also had to learn shorthand, so that they could take letters from dictation. They then had to type them out and take them to the post. A reply would take two days – a bit different from emails today.

For Higher School Certificate I took advanced English and History, French main and Latin subsidiary. It was very hard work, and what made it harder was, because I'd changed schools at the wrong time, I'd been put in the form that didn't learn Latin – and in those days you weren't allowed to take University Entrance in English unless you had an exam pass in Latin. So I had to learn Latin, and learn it fast. I cannot pretend I learnt Latin properly, but I'm a good guesser and that helps. And I do have sympathy with the schoolboy who translated *Sic transit Gloria mundi* as 'Gloria is sick when she travels on Monday' instead of 'Thus passes glory in the world.' But I just managed to scrape the pass mark: 47%.

Every night I would study until ten o'clock. After that I'd go for a walk. I'd walk down the city, across the Market Place, with its shrouded stalls, through the Cathedral Close, and then back home through a network of dark little lanes. It wouldn't be safe to do that now.

There were very few university places in my day – particularly for women. While the men's colleges at Oxford and Cambridge had been established centuries before, the oldest of the women's colleges had been founded only 80 years earlier – and there were just three of them in Oxford and two in Cambridge. Places weren't allocated on results in A levels (HSC) as they are today. Each university set its own separate exam – and, to make matters more difficult for me, both Oxford and Cambridge set their own Latin paper for the arts subjects. Nowadays dozens of new universities have been created, almost all colleges are unisex, with the result that there are so many university places that some of them seem virtually begging people to go there.

While I was slaving away at school, my contemporaries were enjoying life. Most of them had jobs and were earning money they could spend on clothes. The 'New Look' was fashionable, with nipped-in waists (I still had one then) and mid-length skirts. One or two of them had even got married and were swanning elegantly round the city pushing prams. Meanwhile I was bicycling to school in my gymslip – wearing knee socks and a school hat. (I made up for it at weekends. I painted my nails scarlet. I even managed to learn how to smoke and bought a cigarette holder, about a foot long, which I flourished to great effect.)

It's strange how things have changed. I was thought to be an oddity then for staying on at school, and my contemporaries who married were doing the right thing. When I went back to Norwich some 15 years later – when it was my turn to be busy with babies – I met three of them. Their teenaged children were off their hands and it seemed to me that all sorts of possibilities were open to them. Each of them had decided to have another baby.

In the event, I got an interview at both Oxford and Cambridge. At each, the interviewer looked over her half-glasses and remarked, 'Your Latin isn't very good, is it, Miss Upjohn.' And, knowing how awful it was, I shuffled my feet and said 'No it's not.'

(You might not believe this, but it must have been thirty years later that it occurred to me that, if I'd told them I had only been doing it for a year, I might have been accepted. But I wasn't – which turned out to be a good thing.)

One of the things I should like to convince you of, Madison, is that not getting what you want is often much better than getting it. It was for me. The next entrance exam I took was for Royal Holloway College at the University of London, and they, unlike Oxford and Cambridge, didn't have their own Latin paper. And I got a major scholarship which paid all my fees, and even pocket money, for the next three years.

(I am really sorry for university students these days, who have to take out a loan to pay their fees. It must be a terrible burden to start your working life in debt. What's more a degree – particularly an arts degree – doesn't automatically bring you a big income. My first job was on a non-union newspaper (the only one that would have me) and I was paid three pounds a week and had to be a live-in baby-sitter to have a roof over my head. It wasn't until I got a job as an advertising copywriter, three years later, that I

earned enough to have money over and above what I needed to live on. And I stopped full-time work five years after that, so goodness knows how I should have paid it back.)

You might wonder why getting a scholarship was so important, since my parents were comfortable off. But by this time they weren't. And (though I didn't realise it at the time) even if I'd been offered a place at Oxford I don't think I should have been able to take it up. In fact if I hadn't got that scholarship I don't think I should have been able to go to university at all. (I think I've been avoiding telling you the next part of this story.)

When my sister Rosalind was 22 (and I was 16) she got pneumonia. Although she was six years older, I'd always admired her and we were great friends. We had always shared a bedroom, and she used to tell me wonderful stories to make me fall asleep at night. She was very ill and, because there were no antibiotics, it was months and months before she got better. Finally the doctor said she could go back to work. He didn't even send her for an X-ray. (I told you health care was primitive in those days.) However, mass X-rays had started during the war, not for breast cancer as they are today, but for tuberculosis. Later on Rosalind had an X-ray at work. The result showed a patch on her lungs. More tests confirmed that she had TB and, as I told you earlier, the only cure for TB in those days was bed rest and fresh air. TB is very infectious. I reckon I must be very tough not to have got it.

There was a TB sanatorium in Norfolk that was free, but it wasn't thought to be very good – and in any case my parents believed in paying for things. So Rosalind was sent to a private TB sanatorium. She was there for three years. These days I'm sure my parents would have had private health insurance – I don't think it existed then. Private medicine is very expensive – I know how much my new hips cost. After a while she had an operation to collapse part of her lungs. And then she had another to remove part of a rib.

What made it all the more distressing – for me at any rate – was that we weren't allowed to tell anyone about it. It was all part of the old-fashioned belief that you must keep trouble in the family. So I had to make evasive answers when I was asked about Rosalind. I should think some people must have thought she was in a mental hospital or in prison.

Soon there was no money left. My father had retired by then, but his job didn't pay him a pension. It was up to him to save money and invest it wisely, which I'm sure he did. But it also meant he could get his hands on it, and he must have spent it all. So they sold Dorset House, and bought a sweet shop. There were two rooms over the shop, so they sent most of their furniture to auction, and went to live over the shop.

And then, at last, streptomycin, which cures TB, was invented and Rosalind got better. And they knew it had all been worth while. (And you need to know that they were able to sell the shop, buy a house, and have enough money to live happily ever after.) I think my parents were the bravest people I ever met, and it's time to tell you more about them.

CHAPTER 24

Full Circle

You've got a glimpse of my parents as I've been telling you this story, Madison, but – and you might think this is a strange thing to say – I really only got to know them after they were dead. You already know far more about them than I ever did as a child. They didn't make it easy. I had no idea how old my mother and father were. Neither of them would ever have dreamed of telling me. I've also told you how much my father earned. That was a secret, too. And I certainly wasn't told the story of my mother's false teeth. Almost everything I've told you about their early life I've had to find out for myself. I've just had to look at the facts and try to make sense of them. (No wonder I like detective stories.)

But the whole idea of being a parent has changed so dramatically that, to try to let you understand what it was like being a child in those days, I need to tell you about my mother's background and where her ideas came from.

I guess that my mother left school when she was 14. She may have had a job. I have a vague idea she might have worked in a shop called Arding & Hobbs in Clapham Junction – or she might have helped her mother run a houseful of lodgers until she was married at twenty. She once told me she had wanted to be a nurse – I think she would have made a good one – but her mother said the work was so dirty and tiring that she wouldn't let her.

I think she saw herself as a modern woman – you should have heard the tone of her voice when she called something 'early Victorian'. She had her long hair cut off, and wore short skirts. She practised family planning. She wore make-up. She had a vote, though not until 1927 when she turned 30. (*It wasn't until 1928 that women of 21 got the vote in England. In Australia they got it in 1902.*) My father consulted her about everything, and she knew how the family finances were run – unlike most of her contemporaries.

But the most 'modern' thing she did – though not by conscious choice – was to move away from her family circle. After that, I think she was a bit lonely. She must have had a lot of time on her hands, and her coffee-drinking friends were acquaintances and, unlike her sisters, could not be taken into her confidence. But the war changed things for her. When she joined the Red Cross she made a lot of new friends. She thoroughly enjoyed the hospital work with blood donors and loved running the canteen for servicemen at the railway station. I should think she was good at both of them. It got her out of the house, and for the first time it gave her a life outside her own family – and she enjoyed the challenge.

But she had no training for a job, and always felt that her main purpose was to be a wife and mother. She didn't want or expect to go out to work – in fact the opposite. I used to hear men say 'my wife doesn't need to work.' I am sure my mother would have felt she was letting my father down if she had taken a paid job.

Nowadays, it seems, the boot is on the other foot and women are expected to have a job, even when they have small children, and it is those who stay at home who feel they have to justify their decision to look after their own children. The fact that millions of pounds are paid out in childcare subsidies means that a lot of the financial responsibility for looking after little children has passed from their parents to the government, so that what used to be a matter of personal choice – or necessity – has now become a matter of public policy.

I find it terribly sad that so many little children now spend most of their waking hours in a group, being looked after by a succession of trained professionals – who they probably won't see again once they grow up – instead of just pottering about at home with their mothers.

Of course, one of the reasons why so many mothers of small children work full time is that it very often now takes two incomes to support a family. That's something that happened very recently. Back in the 1980s I recall some married friends being indignant because the bank would not take the wife's earnings into consideration when giving them a mortgage – because the expectation was that she would stop working once she had a child.

So they, and others like them, campaigned for a change. At last the lenders gave in, and everyone was happy. But not for long. The law of supply and demand came into effect and, because people could now afford to pay more, houses very soon cost more. So everyone – except the mortgage companies – was worse off. (It doesn't take a mathematical genius to calculate the pressure this puts on women to work – whether or not they have small children, and whether they might prefer to or not). But back to my childhood.

Although my mother liked to think of herself as 'modern' a lot of her ideas stayed the same as her own mother's had been. Children in those days were not encouraged to ask questions, as they are now. They were meant to be seen and not heard – and childhood was supposed to be a time of 'innocence.' In fact it was a time of scary ignorance. There was a huge air of mystery about the whole of the grown-up world. Worst of all was the complete silence about what were then called 'the facts of life'. I was fortunate to be told in advance about menstruation – and that was only because my sister Thelma bullied my mother into it. She hadn't been told, and it had come as a terrifying shock.

One of the deepest mysteries was where babies came from. Today the older children all feel the 'bump' and look forward to the new brother or sister popping out of their mother's tummy. In those days a new baby came as a complete surprise. The day I was born, my sisters went to tea with a family friend. When they came home they were amazed to be told: 'You've got a new sister.' Back in my mother's childhood, once the baby arrived, everyone helped look after it. And with one arriving just about every year, there weren't many theories about how it should be done. You just got on with the job. With a big family, and lots of servants, there would always have been someone around to pick up a baby, and change it, and cuddle it. It might have been comforting, but even so, I wouldn't want to have been born then. Losing six out of fourteen children, as my grandmother did, is hardly a recommendation for child-care.

But, by the time my mother had children of her own, she'd moved a long way away from her family, there weren't nearly so many babies – and there was a completely new set of rules about how they should be looked after.

The man who invented them came from your part of the world – New Zealand – and his name was Sir Frederic Truby King. His book *Feeding and Care of Baby* was published in 1907 and by the time my sisters and I were born, his word was law. He got a knighthood, and later was the first private citizen in New Zealand to be given a State Funeral – so you can tell his views were taken seriously.

Truby King had begun his experimental work with calves, and found that if they were fed at exactly timed intervals and given plenty of fresh air, they thrived. He then applied the same principles to babies. They were to be given plenty of fresh air, fed at strictly four hour intervals (never at night) and left to cry between times. He also

134

advocated a strict regime of toilet training – the calves, presumably, were exempted from this. He believed kissing and cuddling were 'dangerous influences', which should be limited to 'no more than ten minutes a day.' He also opposed higher education for women since 'it was detrimental to their maternal function and hence to the human race.'

But the most damaging of Truby King's ideas were the assumptions he made about the babies themselves. 'Babies are controlling and manipulative from birth and it is necessary to teach them obedience by making them learn that crying will get them nowhere,' he wrote.

It would be interesting to discover what made him ascribe such motives to babies, and to adopt this punitive attitude towards them. 'Spare the rod and spoil the child' seems harsh enough when applied to older children. It's going a bit far to take the same line with babies.

Even if the babies weren't happy, and cried as a result of this regime, Truby King was still on to a winner: 'Crying is necessary to health – essential exercise for the lungs,' he roundly declared.

My mother, modern woman that she was, followed Truby King's teaching enthusiastically. And it worked. I was out of nappies by the time I was a year old. 'Clean and dry, day and night, by twelve months,' she proudly used to tell her friends. She also changed me over from being left-handed to right-handed. (Another of Truby King's bright ideas?) She didn't tell them about the nightmares and the bed-wetting, though the shattering temper tantrums were a bit of an embarrassment – particularly when they happened in public.

She was happy to know she was following the example of the highest in the land. The Duchess of York (who later became Queen Elizabeth when her brother-in-law Edward VIII abdicated) proudly acknowledged that little Princess Elizabeth (who is now Queen Elizabeth II) was 'a Truby King baby.'

I have a mental picture of two contrasting photographs. One is of the Queen greeting little Prince Charles, aged about six, on her return from a long absence abroad. She is shaking him by the hand. The other is of Princess Diana, her eyes alight with love, swooping down to scoop up her boys.

It's hardly surprising, is it, that if you treat your babies as an enemy who is trying to get the better of you, it's almost impossible to establish a loving relationship with them.

Today Australia is agonising with guilt about 'The Stolen Generation' – the hundreds of aboriginal children who were taken away from their mothers by well-intentioned white people. Truby King went one better. He single-handedly separated a whole generation of mothers from their babies – and he did it across three continents.

Fathers didn't read Truby King because – unlike today – they had very little to do with the way their children were brought up. It would have been unthinkable, then, to see a man pushing a pram. And I got to know my father better than my mother. It happened, once more, because people did not get what they wanted. I was a girl instead of a boy.

My father was a very practical man, and I thought that, if I'd been a boy, he would have had someone to help him (every plumber needs a plumber's mate). It struck me that a girl could do this just as capably as a boy – so I did the job. Together we sawed wood and unblocked drains. I passed tools and held ladders. We re-wired the house – it was fascinating to see what went on underneath the floorboards. We put in central heating – a huge job involving a pipe wrench and big iron pipes that had to have a thread put on them. If I hadn't been a third girl, I wouldn't have done any of it. (Being a girl or boy isn't an issue in your family, though I remember you saying that, if your little sister Zoe had been a boy – making four brothers – you'd have left home!)

But my father's great love was clocks. He'd rescue any clock and set it going again. Our house was full of them, and when they all struck at midday and midnight you couldn't hear yourself think. Years later, thanks to brilliant research by Upjohns both here and in America, I discovered that generations of the Upjohns were famous clockmakers. My father was dead by then, and I couldn't tell him. But I'm sure he knows. I don't believe it's too late.

Mercifully, by the time I had children, Truby King had gone out of fashion and Dr Spock had come in. I had scarcely held a baby before I had one of my own. I looked at her and thought: 'How shall I look after you? I haven't read any of the books.' And she looked at me, and I'll swear she said: 'That's all right. I haven't read them either.' So with a bit of common sense, we muddled through together – making mistake after mistake on the way.

There's now enormous pressure on people to be perfect parents, but I sometimes think that muddling through and trying not to make too many mistakes is all you can hope to do. In my day, we were supposed to try to be good children – nowadays people try to be good parents.

A new word 'parenting' has even been invented, and newspapers and magazines devote endless columns to it. But let's face it, the world's not perfect – and a perfect parent would be a disastrous preparation for it. And look on the bright side. If you can't be a Shining Example, you can always be an Awful Warning.

Getting to know your parents is very difficult. The relationship changes so much. At first, you are completely dependent on them. Then the relationship changes year by year. At last, if you're lucky, you recognise each other as likeable adults who can be friends. Not many people make it that far.

I know one or two who are disastrously trapped in their early parent/child relationship. I know a great many who don't understand their parents, don't particularly like them and don't want to have much to do with them. I know one or two who loathe them. And only a few – a happy few – who get it right. At eighteen, you're at the most difficult part of that journey, and sometimes you'll find – like Alice in *Through the Looking Glass* – that you have to set off in what looks like the opposite direction in order to reach your destination.

But for me, as I said at the beginning of this chapter, I have – at long last – finally got to know mine, and to recognise what wonderful people they were, and how lucky I was to have them as my parents. And it's all thanks to you, Madison. I thought, when I was writing this book, that I was giving you a present. Instead, I find it's you who have given one to me. But that's always the way.

So this is all I've got left to tell you:

It's never too late.